Soul Survivors

Soul Survivors

The Wigan Casino Story

Russ Winstanley
and
David Nowell

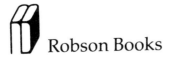

Robson Books

First published in Great Britain in 1996 by Robson Books
Ltd. This edition published 1997 by Robson Books Ltd.,
Bolsover House, 5-6 Clipstone Street, London W1P 8LE

British Library Cataloguing in Publication Data
A catalogue record for this title is available from the British
Library

ISBN 1 86105 126 3

Book design by Harold King

Photoset in North Wales by Derek Doyle Associates,
Mold, Flintshire. Printed in Great Britain by St
Edmundsbury Press, Bury St Edmunds, Suffolk.

To my long-suffering wife Jacky, who helped type the manuscript. And to our 'soul kids', Michelle and Michael, all-nighter-goers of the future.

Dave Nowell

This memory-filled dedication to the irreplaceable Wigan Casino could not have been possible without the guidance and help of my much loved mother, Bette, and my late father, Bert; my wonderful wife, Doreen, and delightful daughters, Jodie and Dionne (not forgetting little Russie); Val, Gil and Myles and the friendship of Mandy and Tom Hunt; the thousands of friendships with Northern Soul lovers who helped create a legend and are now re-launching our sensational scene; the memory of four much missed personalities who meant so much to everyone at the heart of Soul; Casino owner, Gerry Marshall; manager, Mike Walker; DJs Kenny Spence and Mike Rollo. God bless you all.

Russ Winstanley

Acknowledgements

The authors would like to thank the following for their invaluable help in putting together this book: the *Wigan Observer*, the *Blackpool Evening Gazette*, Ian Palmer of *Manifesto* and Pep of *Soul Times, Blues and Soul, The Face*, Trevor Smith of Smith's in Wigan, and photographer Dave Motler. And, of course, the former Casino regulars who contributed their highly entertaining memories of the greatest dance club in history.

The photos of the Casino's DJs, of stars Tommy Hunt and Major Lance and of two of the all-nighters were taken by Russ Winstanley; of the Casino Classic staff by Doreen Winstanley and of the authors on the site today by Jodie Winstanley.

Contents

Preface

The music died for thousands of Northern Soul fans on 6 December 1981. That was the day the Casino Club in Wigan closed its doors for the last time to await demolition.

For eight years the Casino's weekly all-night dance marathons attracted thousands of dancers, record company bosses, journalists and camera crews, film-makers, and more than a little controversy.

In the early days the Casino was merely meeting the demand of a growing legion of underground music fanatics. Northern Soul fans demanded fast, black American soul music – and the rarer the better.

Despite the initial reluctance of the Casino's owner, Gerry Marshall, the venue threw open its doors to the soul fraternity at 2 a.m. on 23 September 1973.

The DJs, staff and enthusiasts were hoping only to stage a successful, trouble-free event. Instead they created a 'monster' which grew and grew and became an institution for thousands of youngsters.

The Casino legend not only influenced the national pop charts but spawned its own record label and magazine.

In 1977 a TV documentary on the club was watched by millions, and the following year the American music magazine *Billboard* voted the Casino the world's best disco – beating among others the then trendy Studio 54 in New York.

In the mid to late 70s there was hardly a single Briton under the age of 30 who had not been to the Casino, knew someone who had, or was at the very least aware of its legendary all-night dance marathons.

By the time the club was tragically forced to close in 1981, it

1

THE WIGAN CASINO SOUL CLUB

PROUDLY PRESENTS

RUSS' EVERYSOUND DISCO

PLUS

IAN AND FRIENDS

ALL NIGHTER

2 a.m. to 8 a.m. EVERY SATURDAY (Sun. morn.)
STARTING SAT. SEPT. 22 - ADMISSION 75p.

HEAR THE COUNTRY'S TOP RAREST SOUNDS AT THE ALLNIGHTER THAT WILL SOON BECOME THE COUNTRY'S BEST

Everyone should get in as the club hold's about 1,500 and is in the Town Centre with plenty of parking nearby.

LOTS OF FOOD AND SOFT DRINKS, etc.

FIRST NIGHT BADGES

will be made for the **EXACT** number of people wanting them. Don't miss out!

You **HAVE TO** be a member for at least 48 hours before the club opens, so fill in the form to arrive not later than Thursday, September 20th and your FREE membership card will be waiting for you. The "Feds" say **no admission** without membership, so you've been warned. If you don't want to cut the magazine, send the same details in block letters to the address given.

Post to: **WIGAN CASINO SOUL CLUB, STATION ROAD, WIGAN WN1 1YQ, LANCASHIRE**
W.C.S.C. APPLICATION FORM FOR MEMBERSHIP

I (name) ....

of (address) ....
....

do apply for membership to Wigan Casino Soul Club. I am over 18 years of age and agree to abide by the rules of the club.

✶ APPLICATION TO ARRIVE NOT LATER THAN THURSDAY, SEPTEMBER 20th ✶

had more than 100,000 members. And those who attended those crushed, emotion-packed final nights would swear that nearly every single member turned up to pay their final respects.

After the Casino's closure, the Northern Soul scene went underground again, attracting a smaller though no less dedicated crowd. But now, more than twenty years after it first opened its doors, thousands of soul fans are once again enjoying dancing to, and collecting, the music of their youth. And Northern Soul has become truly international, with its infectious music spreading to Belgium, Spain and Germany.

Many former Casino-goers, now a little heavier and often considerably greyer, are renewing lost friendships, enjoying once again the music of black America and rediscovering the atmosphere of an era that many thought had gone for ever. Packed all-nighters drawing up to 1,500 new-breed and old-breed soul fans are taking place in, for example, Keele in Staffordshire, the 100 Club in London and the Ritz in Manchester.

So what is it that makes family men and women, many in their thirties and forties, pack their holdalls and drive hours down the motorway to take part in the Northern Soul experience? Why in the techno age of the 1990s, do so many people prefer the music put out by obscure labels in America in the 1960s?

Rave or dance music is the modern disco sound to teenagers and under-thirties in Britain today. Its followers travel huge distances to dance to the music they love, often falling foul of the law. Sounds familiar?

To those new-breed rave dancers who may wonder about the origins of their own dance scene, and to the former Wigan crowd who were part of a magical era, this book attempts to recount the phenomenon of the Casino and Northern Soul.

Introduction:
Come and Get These Memories

So what on earth is Northern Soul, and how did it get its peculiar name? The short answer is that the term was originally coined to describe 'rare soul of the type enjoyed in the north of England'. But what used to be called Northern Soul has spread so far and wide, throughout Britain and on to the Continent, that the term is nowadays somewhat misleading. Rare soul is probably a more accurate phrase now, because the music that has spanned three decades has become truly international. Even so, Northern Soul, or rare soul, has its roots in the mod scene in Britain in the 1960s.

Jazz, blues and gospel had all been long-established forms of music in black America when rock 'n' roll heralded a new era of commercialism in the late 1950s. Racism and oppression of black Americans and their culture were still very much alive in many parts of America. Some radio stations would not play records by black artists. Some would not even play records by Elvis Presley in the early days because they thought he sounded too black. But many white traditionalists had to rethink their musical attitudes when a guy called Berry Gordy Jr founded the empire that was to become the Tamla Motown phenomenon.

The Detroit-based Motown empire grew from humble origins to a multi-million-dollar business that produced commercially successful soul records by black artists on a scale that had never been seen before. The Miracles ('Shop Around'), the Marvelettes ('Please, Mr Postman') and Mary Wells ('My Guy') were among the artists who gave Motown its early hits in 1961.

When the Holland/Dozier/Holland hit factory swung into

full production with artists like the Supremes, the Four Tops, Marvin Gaye, 'Little' Stevie Wonder, the Temptations, the Contours, Edwin Starr, the Detroit Spinners, Martha Reeves and the Vandellas, the worldwide hits went on and on.

The American output of the Motown sound come on a variety of labels, like Tamla, Motown, Soul and Gordy. In Britain, to the delight of mods and pop fans, those thousands of recordings were consolidated for the most part on the Tamla Motown label.

Motown's success was, and still is, enormous and made household names of many of its stars. Inevitably it spawned many imitators, some successful and other outright flops. The Atlantic and Stax labels were highly successful and had their own distinctive sound, boasting between them such soul giants as Aretha Franklin and Otis Redding.

For many soul fans, those recordings of the mid-1960s were the epitome of soul music. Music dripping with emotion, with powerful vocals, blaring horns and massive orchestration; or sparsely produced with a heavy bass line and a wailing vocal. But all of it had to have that magic ingredient … soul.

Although ballads were part and parcel of soul music, the British clubgoer demanded soul with an up-tempo dance beat. It could be a stomping beat, as in the Four Tops' 'Reach Out, I'll Be There', or more floating, like Jackie Wilson's 'I Get the Sweetest Feeling'. But danceability was essential.

The late 1960s and early 1970s saw a period of change in American soul music. A 'softer' sound was coming in, which gradually became the more sophisticated 1970s soul, or funk. Whereas many British soul fans liked the funkier sounds of James Brown, Earth Wind and Fire, and Kool and the Gang, some northern clubs stuck with the traditional 1960s music.

Dave Godin, a columnist with *Blues and Soul* magazine, is credited with coining the phrase Northern Soul, to differentiate between the music enjoyed by northern and southern club-goers at that time.

This massive musical following resulted in Northern Soul nights opening up in various parts of the North and Midlands in venues as varied as working men's clubs, youth clubs and regular discos. The Twisted Wheel in Manchester was one of the first to host all-night soul sessions, drawing fans from far and wide. The music played was often new-release or recent Motown, Stax and Atlantic material, but slowly and surely the new-release material started to dry up as American labels went for a 'funkier' sound.

Northern Soul DJs started to look back in time for their 'new' material. As long as the record was new to the dancers and had the required ingredients, it didn't matter if it was already a few years old.

Many soul labels had released quality material which got overlooked or under-promoted in the Motown/Atlantic/Stax-dominated 1960s. Indeed, even today much unreleased and long-forgotten Motown material is emerging, to be snapped up by collectors and CD-buyers alike. Many small labels went bust. Labels like Okeh, Cameo Parkway, Ric Tic, Revilot, Capitol and RCA had thousands of hours' worth of classic soul music that fitted the northern criteria.

It was those labels, and many more obscure ones, that the British DJs and collectors targeted. Often trips to the USA were required to hunt down such sounds in second-hand shops and the vaults of defunct labels. But the expense was more than worth it if the DJ unearthed a handful of class tunes. Their value could soon be ten, twenty or a hundred times what the DJ paid for it if the record proved popular in the clubs at home.

When the Wheel closed, due partly to drug problems, there were other clubs willing to continue the Northern Soul tradition. Va-Va's in Bolton, the Catacombs in Wolverhampton and – best of all – the Torch in Stoke-on-Trent enticed dancers from all over the country.

And so the seeds of the scene which continues to this day were born. Driving sometimes hundreds of miles to a venue, hitchhiking or enduring interminable train and bus journeys became part of the Northern Soul fans' lifestyle. All-night venues were alcohol-free and trouble-free. Dancers packed holdalls with several changes of clothes to stay fresh during the mammoth dance sessions of six or eight hours. Rare records were changing hands for large amounts of money as collecting previously unheard-of soul gems became an obsession for many dancers.

Slowly but surely, at many clubs the classic Motown/Atlantic/Stax sounds were replaced by Northern Soul 'discoveries', which soon became classics in their own right among the knowledgeable dancers. Some DJs, keen to protect the identity of an exclusive record which guaranteed them work and a cult following, began 'covering up' their rarities. They would literally cover the record label with tape so that the title and artist were obscured, and invent fictitious names for such songs (for example, 'Double Cookin' ' by the Checkerboard Squares became 'Strings a Go Go' by the Bob Wilson Sounds). It was only a matter of time before the real identity of a record leaked out, but it all added to the mystique and fun at the time.

Such bizarre goings-on were bound sooner or later to make great newspaper and magazines copy. And the spectacularly athletic dancers would make fine pictures and TV footage. The Northern Soul media explosion finally happened in the early 1970s, and changed or influenced the musical tastes of a generation of youngsters.

Part I

Early Days and Late Nights

1

Countdown – Here I Come

The year was 1973. Britain had a Tory prime minister, Edward Heath, a pint of beer cost as little as 12p, Roger Moore had just made his first James Bond film, *Live and Let Die*, and a twenty-three-day cruise on the *Canberra* could be yours for the princely sum of £170. Gary Glitter and Slade were rocking the country's teenagers, kids were swooning over Donny Osmond, while mums and dads preferred the melodic tones of Perry Como and John Denver.

In the north of England, however, something was happening. An underground movement that cared nothing for the trends of the day was slowly gathering momentum and preparing to explode into the consciousness of people all over Britain, and even Europe and America. Northern Soul fans, already stuck in a 1960s timewarp, were growing in number and constantly searching for new atmospheric venues in which to listen and dance to their own 'private' music. But that music, which had been around since the magical Tamla Motown heyday of the mid- to late 1960s, was about to go public in a big way, due in no small measure to an incredible venue called the Casino Club in Wigan.

One of the men who played a major role in setting up what was to become *the* youth phenomenon of the 1970s was a soul fan and DJ called Russ Winstanley. Wigan-born Russ got a taste for show business with one of the biggest local bands, Rainbow

Cottage. He used to work as a roadie for the group and also helped with backing vocals. That was in 1967 and 1968, and two years later his love of music led him into DJing at local pubs and clubs. Russ started out with another local lad, John Lowe, and in those days he played a mixed bag of heavy rock, oldies and soul. Gradually the soul sounds started to take over, and Russ became an avid fan and collector of soul records.

By 1971 Russ and others were starting to go to the legendary Blackpool Mecca's Highland Room to hear the latest rare 'monsters' from the likes of Ian Levine, Keith Minshull and Tony Jebb. At the same time the popular Torch all-nighters in Stoke were running and attracting increasing numbers of soul devotees from all over the country.

As Russ recalls: 'I only went to the Torch a couple of times. I much preferred Blackpool Mecca. The Mecca's sound system wasn't sparkling, but the atmosphere was amazing. I immediately felt one of the lads and got caught up in the atmosphere. There was just a cacophony of noise, of records I had never heard before. I remember hearing the Crusaders' "Put It Where You Want It" and asking what it was.'

Northern Soul had a big following in the Wigan area and Russ started featuring at places like the Wigan Bier Keller, the Riverside Club and Wigan Rugby Club. His original partner, John Lowe, moved to Jersey, so it was Russ alone who moved on to Newtown British Legion.

He began to earn a good reputation for his taste in music and kept up the visits to Blackpool Mecca in his search for the latest sounds: 'I remember buying "Out on the Floor" off Tony Jebb for £2 and it was re-released costing £1 the week after.'

Russ got much of his collection from Select-a-Disc in Nottingham, and was also fortunate enough to have an uncle who lived in Fort Lauderdale, Florida. He used to send Russ packs of records, having been dispatched to scour junk and second-hand shops with a list of in-demand labels which his nephew told him were likely to produce Northern Soul gems.

The Torch's controversial reign was about to come to an end, as a result of various problems, including drugs, and Russ wondered if an all-nighter could be staged in the Wigan area. He immediately thought of the Casino Club in Station Road, a huge First World War building with a massive dancefloor and a capacity of around 1,500. It also had an adjoining sister club, Mr M's, which could also hold several hundred. Together, that meant a lot of people!

The Casino, or the 'Emp' as it was known to Wiganers, had been close to the hearts of local people since it was built by the Atherton Brothers. Part of it was later converted to the second-largest billiard hall in the country.

Around the time of the Second World War, Eddie Farrimond became the owner and in the heyday of dance bands the Palais (later Mr M's) was added. In the 1960s Howcroft Brewery took it over and changed the name to the Casino. Cabaret reigned in the Palais and beat groups in the Casino. Local businessman Gerry Marshall took over in the late 1960s, assisted by management Mike Walker and Harry Green in the 1970s.

Among the top names who had appeared at the club before 1973 were Tom Jones, Shirley Bassey, Herman's Hermits, David Bowie and the Rolling Stones. But times were changing. As Russ said: 'I had never worked at the Casino because it was mostly handled by agencies, but I had been in a few times. In 1973 it was the end of cabaret in Mr M's and they were struggling a little bit.'

Casino manager Mike Walker was a big soul fan and he and Russ approached Gerry Marshall about the possibility of staging an all-nighter in September 1973. Russ did not get an encouraging response from his first approach: 'Gerry virtually chucked me out of his office. Mike Walker helped to talk him round, and after a few ifs and buts he said, "OK, you put the event on and handle the adverts and promotion and we will go 50/50 on it." '

Russ placed a £55 full-page advert in *Blues and Soul* magazine, which virtually every Northern Soul fan read, and got ready for the event. Russ was then DJing with Ian Fishwick and the event (admission 75p) was billed as 'Russ and Ian'. ('A lot of people might have thought it was Ian Levine,' Russ now

WIGAN CASINO
ALLNIGHTER
Every Sat / Sun morning 2am-8am

1st ANNIVERSARY
ALLNIGHTER
Sat Night / Sun morning 2am-10am
(2 extra hours)

SEPTEMBER 21st

To express our overwhelming gratitude
to you we are
going to present to all our members

BRITAIN'S BIGGEST AND BEST SOUL NIGHT EVER HELD

featuring Britain's Top Soul D.J.'s

RUSS, RICHARD, KEV, MARTIN plus **PEP,
JOHN VINCENT, KEITH MINSHULL, FRANK**

plus other top guest D.J.s.

Playing the greatest sounds old or new, very rare
or just rare!

Over £500 worth of prizes to be given away, hundreds
of records, cassette tape recorders, etc.

★ TOP NORTHERN DANCE COMPETITION ★
£50 1st prize ★ £30 2nd prize ★ £15 3rd prize

Everyone with a ticket will receive a brilliant new free 'Souvenir' badge only to be issued on the night

TICKETS ON SALE PRICE £1.50p + SAE

(MEMBERS ONLY) (STRICTLY LIMITED)   DON'T MISS OUT—EVERYONE'S COMING!!!

TO JOIN OUR CLUB, SEND FORM BELOW TO ARRIVE AT LEAST 48 HOURS BEFORE YOU DO

Post to: WIGAN CASINO SOUL CLUB, STATION ROAD, WIGAN WN1 1YQ, LANCASHIRE
W.C.S.C. APPLICATION FORM FOR MEMBERSHIP

I (name) ....

of (address) ....

do apply for membership to Wigan Casino Soul Club. I am over 18 years of age and agree to abide by the
rules of the club.

P.S. Don't forget Beachcomber Soul Snack Bar open from 12 midnight—2a.m. and from 8a.m.—10a.m. for breakfasts (adj. Casino entrance) reflects.) Gerry Marshall closed the 'normal' Saturday night Casino event at 12.30am on 23 September and the club got ready for the 2am start of the all-nighter.

The Sherries' 'Put Your Loving Arms Around Me' was first on the turntable as the club opened its doors and 652 people poured in. Russ provided the sounds for virtually the whole night until 8am, apart from a few breaks when Ian Fishwick took over.

'That first night was so amazing I couldn't have fallen asleep if I had tried,' said Russ. 'At the time I was earning about £12 a week. From that one night we made £400. I couldn't believe it. I went to see Gerry at the end of the night and reminded him he had said 50/50 and he said, "you're not having half of that. I'll give you £50 a night for doing it." That was a hell of a lot of money in those days, so I agreed. I was still getting £50 a night in 1981.'

Russ, however, was allowed to sell records from the upstairs record bar, so with the spin-off business he wasn't unhappy with the deal.

Attendance at the club rose steadily as its reputation grew and by the first anniversary all-nighter in September 1974 the Casino was so packed that its sister club, Mr M's, was opened to take the overflow. Mr M's soon became a firm favourite in its own right, with its own DJ line-up, and so the legend and capacity of the Casino all-nighters grew and grew.

Youngsters with holdalls and noisy cassette recorders started to become a common sight around town centres in the North-West, and much further afield, on Saturday nights. As drunks poured out of pubs and into bus stations and railway stations to weave their way home after their nights out, soul fans were just getting going. In many towns within a reasonable distance of Wigan, they would emerge at 11.30pm, midnight or even later to catch the last bus or train to the 'Heart of Soul'. Others hired cars and organized coach trips, often travelling hundreds of miles to arrive in Wigan for the 2am start of their weekly over-indulgence of rare soul music.

The chatter and banter among devotees would become

excited as adrenalin started to flow in anticipation of the night ahead. Journeys to the Casino often proved to be a major part of the fun of attending the all-nighters, and by the time the average soul fan had trekked through the darkened streets of Wigan for ten or fifteen minutes from the bus or train station, it was impossible to believe that anything other than a memorable event lay ahead.

The scene outside the club was at the same time exciting and overawing to anyone seeing it for the first time. The seemingly huge Casino building dominated Station Road. Wherever you looked there were people in their mid-teens, late teens, twenties, thirties and even forties milling around in the darkness. A constant flow of cars, coaches and minibuses entered the club's two main car parks, discharging more and more people to join the crowds already there.

The fashions of the day were long trench coats – often leather – baggy 32-inch flares and brogues or loafers. The coats would later be stripped off to reveal vests or flared-collared T-shirts. Girls favoured leather trench coats too and also wore loose-fitting long, strappy dresses (which would flare out when

RUSS' MAIL ORDER SERVICE

If you want regular lists of the great sounds we play here, plus the latest pressings —then drop me a large S.A.E.

RUSS' MONSTER IMPORTS
10 BAYTREE ROAD, WIGAN WN6 7RT

Telephone Wigan 34070

Also
Wigan Market every Saturday

Also on sale at the All Nighter

WIGAN CASINO

Soul Club Ladies

17

dancing) or sometimes cheesecloth shirts, or something similar, and denim skirts or jeans.

Most dancers carried a holdall with a change of clothes to throw on during or after the all-nighter. Bags, flat caps and berets sported sew-on badges proclaiming 'Wigan Casino – Heart of Soul', 'Night Owl', 'The Torch Lives On' or 'The Twisted Wheel'.

The three-storey Casino building was dominated by a huge illuminated sign saying simply 'Casino Club'. (Over the years a few letters went out, never to be repaired, so the Cas Club was all you got.) Colourful posters advertising forthcoming all-nighters were plastered on the front of the building.

Next to the Casino was one of the luckiest café owners in Britain. Pre-1973 this small, simple place was probably used to catering for just a trickle of late-night customers from the ABC cinema opposite and the odd drunk staggering home. Suddenly he found himself next to the biggest youth attraction in the area, and must have pinched himself to see if he was dreaming. The enterprising owner rose to the occasion admirably and seized the opportunity provided by the advent of the all-nighters to stay open until the early hours. The place was always packed on a Saturday night, particularly in winter, when frozen soul fans would cram into the café for a 'warm'.

Another shrewd operator was the owner of the hot dog stand, who also enjoyed busy nights in Station Road.

The original 2am opening time in the first few years meant a lengthy wait for most fans dependent on public transport, and the portable cassettes once again proved their worth as dancers waited for the doors to open. Impatient soul fans sometimes took to dancing on the pavement or in the car parks to the fast-tempo music being dished out into the night.

As 2am approached, the number of fans outside the club swelled. So did the number of uniformed police, and on particularly busy nights one-way Station Road was virtually impassable. On occasions officers with dogs came to literally herd fans off the road and on to the pavement. Station Road wasn't wide or long enough to accommodate 2,000 soul fans without a great number spilling into the road. Orderly queues were not the fashion and it was a case of every man for himself.

Quickly the numbers near the two double doors at the front of the Casino would grow until the crush was 50 yards long and a dozen or more deep. As opening time neared, you could find yourself firmly pinned in the middle of a huge swaying crowd only 8 feet or so from the door but with no chance of moving other than with the mob.

Holdall pinned to your chest, you would wait for the surge before the doors opened. People could occasionally be heard screaming as they were pinned against a wall. To ironic laughter (because no one could move even if they wanted to) someone would shout, 'Move back, will you? He's trapped.' You could find yourself literally suspended in midair by the crush. And then at last the doors would open and the doormen would vainly shout things like, 'Stop Pushing' and 'Get Back', as they tried to let in only a few fans at a time, leaning against the crowd threatening to overwhelm them.

People were often so firmly sandwiched together that they had to be dragged inside the club by the dinner-jacketed bouncers. Often you found yourself gratefully inside the brightly lit reception area minus your holdall, which would come tumbling in with the next group of gasping bodies. If all this sounds a bit frightening, well, it sometimes was, and this was one reason why the all-nighters later began at 12.30am, thereby avoiding the build-up of such huge numbers outside the club.

That people were prepared to put up with such discomfort just to get into the Casino was a testament to the drawing power of the club. Frequently, particularly when a live act was performing, you had to get there early and brave the crush just to make sure you got in. The stream of customers through the front door sometimes went on beyond 4 or 5am, and on occasions there was a lock-out.

What was so special about an ageing, cavernous nightclub, in Wigan of all places? Up till then, Wigan's main claims to fame were Uncle Joe's Mint Balls, Wigan Pier and a decent rugby team, but image-wise it could not compete with trendier towns and cities such as London, Liverpool and Manchester. The answer is twofold. First, the music: Northern Soul was, and still is, uniquely exciting and enjoys a fanatical cult following, and visitors to the Casino were assured of hearing many rare records that were not being played anywhere else. And second, the Casino itself: it had character, it had charisma, and above all it had an unrivalled atmosphere.

One of the most refreshing aspects of the Casino was its total lack of dress restrictions at a time when many 'normal' venues were preaching that it was smart to be smart and, sorry, no groups of lads tonight. In your local Mecca it was probably jacket and tie essential, couples only please, and don't look the wrong way at the door staff. In some clubs, taking your jacket off *inside* the club was a chucking-out offence, and the accent was on sophistication, chicken in a basket and lads standing around drinking and leering, while the girls danced around their handbags. The sight of a bloke dancing at all, let alone without a girl opposite him, was a relative rarity and usually drew stares.

At the Casino anything went – jeans, cords, boots, trainers, shorts, whatever. A party of blokes could literally have turned up in their underpants and gained admission as long as they had membership cards. Certainly on hot summer nights no one looked twice at a bloke in Bermuda shorts showing off his suntan on the dancefloor. Even in the middle of winter the heat generated inside the club was such that many male dancers were bare-chested, as the condensation misted up the mirrors and ran down the walls like water.

Inside and out of the Casino the punters weren't treated like schoolchildren. You could sit or lie on the floor (and many did through exhaustion or simply because there were no spare chairs), curl up and go to sleep, stand on the tables, drink a can of beer from your holdall, or tape your favourite soul sounds or live act on your cassette recorder.

For those who never went to the Casino, the best way to describe its main hall is (forgive us, Mr Marshall) as a sort of downmarket Blackpool Tower Ballroom. The huge maplewood sprung dancefloor dominated the club and a high balcony circled the floor until it met the large stage. Furniture was simple – basic wooden chairs and tables were scattered around and were always full. The carpet was threadbare in parts and usually littered with cigarette stubs and discarded chewing gum. The early-twentieth-century building felt old and a bit dank. Soft drinks – all that was on sale at the all-nighters – were drunk straight from the bottle.

Visitors to the Casino would enter through the brightly lit ground-floor entrance and climb a dozen carpetless steps to the cash desk. Membership card checked, money handed over and ticket issued, the ticket would then be torn by a bouncer standing to the right of the counter. At a 45-degree angle to the right, a flight of steps wound up, levelled out and then turned sharp right again to finish above your head. Anyone standing at that point in the early hours on a Sunday morning would have witnessed a constant procession of eager bag-carrying soul fans, most of them chewing gum, moving past for several hours to come, their footsteps clumping on the hard floor.

The sound of loud music and chatter became stronger as you climbed the steep steps. On the first-floor landing was the manager's office, to the front and right. A pair of swing doors would burst open every few seconds just beyond it, giving a tantalizing first glimpse of the darkened Casino dancefloor.

The stairs continued upwards to the balcony and the upstairs cloakroom, and this was often the first port of call for Casino-goers. The temperature in the club was usually rising fast by the time you pushed open the top set of swing doors and stepped into the heat of the all-nighter. Sometimes it was like entering a sauna.

Anyone coming through the top doors would find themselves in the bottom left-hand corner of the upper floor of the huge, high-ceiling Empress Hall. In front was a short, sharp flight of steps leading to the top-level cloakroom. On the right was a huge mirrored bar, behind which were stacks of Coke bottles in crates and, nearer to the door through which you had just entered, a small counter selling hot drinks, cigarettes, pasties, etc.

The simple food could hardly be described as *haute cuisine*. Hardened pies and pasties seemed to linger in the heated display

WE ARE <u>NOT</u> CLOSING DOWN

WELL, THAT'S THE END OF ONE STUPID RUMOUR ABOUT

THE WIGAN CASINO
SOUL ALL-NIGHTER

We've never said we're the country's best. Everyone has their own opinions. We do know that we play some brilliant sounds and we think that we have the fastest-growing membership of any club in the country. So come along yourself and find out why. There's no fear of us beihg 'blacked out' as we have our own generator.

EVERY SAT. NIGHT/SUN. MORNING 2 a.m. - 8 a.m.

FEATURING

RUSS' EVERYSOUND DISCO

PLUS

KEV ROBERTS

And top guest D.J.'s playing the top sounds (ask anyone!)

To join our club, send the form below to arrive at least 48 hours before you do. Please send s.a.e. — or you can pick up your free membership card at our reception.

Post to: **WIGAN CASINO SOUL CLUB, STATION ROAD, WIGAN WN1 1YQ, LANCASHIRE**
W.C.S.C. APPLICATION FORM FOR MEMBERSHIP

I (name) ....

of (address) ....

do apply for membership to Wigan Casino Soul Club. I am over 18 years of age and agree to abide by the rules of the club.

cabinet for ever and those brave few who tried them usually drew strange looks. Tea and coffee came in polystyrene cups and you had to help yourself to sugar from a bowl – after waiting your turn for the one or two plastic spoons thoughtfully provided for the 2,000 dancers.

In front of the bar, the spacious area around the balcony would always be packed with soul fans chatting, queuing for the bar or tea bar, or swapping records. A single row of wooden tables surrounded the balcony's edge, all of which were constantly full and piled with bags, drinks and the inevitable portable cassette recorders.

Any first-time Casino visitor who managed to battle his or her way to the balcony and peer over the edge could not fail to be impressed with the sight below. Some 15 feet or so down there would be a sea of moving bodies, so many in number and so tightly packed in the early hours that it was at times impossible to see where the dancefloor ended and the tables began. A seemingly long way away was the stage, with its huge dark curtains drawn, and at the front of the curtains stood the DJ among the sound decks and records stacked in boxes and milk crates.

In front and about 3 feet below him was one of the largest and best-kept dancefloors in the country. As far as the eye could see, soul fans gyrated to the loud, crashing music under the two simple fluorescent lights suspended from the ceiling. These were virtually the only forms of lighting, apart from the small red wall-lights and the white 'Exit' signs illuminated in the doorways, and it always took the eyes a few seconds to adjust.

The atmosphere was always electric, and the sense of occasion so strong that you could almost reach out and touch it. This was no run-of-the-mill nightclub where people were so pissed that they didn't know or care whether they were at the Locarno or the British Legion. This was no trendy disco where a teenager could wander in, order a pint, eye up the women and say, 'These places are all the same.' This was Wigan Casino, and it had an aura about it that was undeniable.

All around, northern accents mingled with Scots, Geordie,

Cockney, Yorkshire and Black Country. Many of the dancers had made journeys of three, four or more hours to listen to the music they loved and be with people they wanted to be with – often from the other side of the country. It was at the same time both amusing and fascinating to get chatting to a stranger from, say, Scotland and find you had mutual acquaintances from the South, Midlands and North who all frequented the Casino. It would be an overstatement to say that everybody knew everybody else, but certainly many hundreds of Casino regulars would see many hundreds of friends at any all-nighter.

Energy and this sense of common purpose exuded from the place. The knowledgeable soul crowd would simultaneously clap at certain punchy parts of many records and there would be spontaneous applause for any DJ who spun a particularly well-liked rare soul gem.

As the night wore on, getting around the place became more and more tricky, and even hazardous. Those who could not last the pace of the eight-hour marathons (and let's face it, that's as long as the average working day) slumped across tables, in corners on chairs or on makeshift beds of holdalls. As you groped around for your holdall in the dark, a misplaced foot would sometimes be met with a grunt and you would realize you had just ruined someone's beauty sleep by standing on his head.

Condensation hung in the air – it was impossible even to stand still without sweating – so this was no club for poseurs. Looking 'cool' was almost impossible and fans hoping to find some respite from the heat fared little better, and maybe even worse, in Mr M's.

The former cabaret club, named after owner Mr Marshall, was opened as an 'overflow' room early in the history of the all-nighters, but soon it took on its own identity. Usually opening from 3am until 7am (an hour before the long night drew to a close), Mr M's was much smaller and more compact than the Empress Hall. Its capacity was around 600 or 700, giving the weekly soul events a total capacity of around 2,000.

As with the Casino itself, Mr M's was dominated by an

oblong-shaped dancefloor which stretched almost its entire length. A low balcony surrounded the room.

Dancers entering Mr M's through one of two sets of swing doors emerged at the front, next to the stage from where the DJs fed the sounds to the soul-hungry crowd. If anything, Mr M's tended to be more claustrophobic than the main room. The dancefloor ended where the seating booths and their leather-backed chairs began, so anyone coming into the packed upstairs club had to skirt the floor and run the gauntlet of dancing, jumping and spinning bodies.

Mr M's was better lit, more compact and cosier than the main floor, and where the Casino would play a mix of 'new' and 'old' records, Mr M's specialized in oldies only and had its own line-up of DJs.

Access to the balcony was gained by two narrow carpeted stairways. The balcony was usually dark and packed with soul fans in prime viewing positions overlooking the crowded dancefloor. There was no dancefloor upstairs, but that didn't stop enthusiastic dancers from wearing a hole in the carpet.

The very best Northern Soul is often frantic, energetic and emotional, and the dancing style of its followers mirrors this. Athletic dancers would glide swiftly around the floor and then suddenly kick out a leg and go into a backdrop or the splits. Those with brilliant coordination and balance could then leap up and go into the sort of fast spin an ice skater would be proud of. Handstands and somersaults were sometimes seen and the top dancers could combine many of those moves in the course of a record.

Since the best Northern Soul dancers were fast, supple and acrobatic, they were a joy to behold and many entertaining hours could be spent simply peering down from the balconies to watch.

Although there was an element of competitiveness among the dancers, the atmosphere out on the floor was friendly. When dancers accidentally clashed, stood on each other's feet or hurtled into someone after mistiming a spin, it was generally accompanied by a quick 'Sorry, mate.' Even so, it could be daunting for a youngster making his debut on the Casino dancefloor, and there was a fairly obvious kind of pecking order in the club. The better dancers were usually found at the front, near the stage, and it sometimes took newcomers months or even years before they dared to trespass on that territory!

After a few hours in the sauna-like heat, soul fans usually found it necessary to change their clothes, or at least put on a fresh top. Some got changed where they stood, spraying Brut liberally under the armpits, and others trotted off to join the multitudes in the toilets.

The gents' toilets were basic and owed more to public conveniences than de-luxe nightclub loos. The cubicles were basic and graffiti-ridden and the sinks were often blocked. On occasions something would spring a leak and in the Casino's dying months you could splash into the toilets through a thin puddle of water. There was also the unsettling prospect of sitting on the loo and having the door kicked in by a bouncer. You would stare at him with your trousers around your ankles, wondering how to begin the conversation, and he would move on to another cubicle if he was satisfied that a major drugs deal was not in progress. Even more unnerving would be sounds of scuffling from another cubicle and shouts of 'Get off me, you bastard' as the occupant was unceremoniously dragged off to the manager's office or wherever. However, the toilets were most frequently used as changing rooms, and bags and bodies would ring the room as blokes rubbed themselves down, had a wash and put on fresh clothes.

Although many girls and women went to the Casino, couples were a rare sight and there was little or no snogging in corners. Anyone going to the club expecting to see drug addicts and lust-crazed couples in dark corners would have been sadly disappointed. (Having said that, there were one or two blokes who claimed to have enjoyed some passion on the darkened balcony of Mr M's!)

It would be an exaggeration to say that sex was definitely *out* at the all-nighters. Before and after, fine, but *during*, no. The few couples who did go to the Casino kept a decent distance from each other. Occasionally a girl would be seen sitting on a bloke's knee, but it seemed somehow out of place in the surroundings. People went to the Casino for the music, the dancing and the company, and it felt somehow disrespectful to spend all night, or even part of it, staring lovingly into someone's eyes, thus ignoring the event taking place around you. Compare that with the average pop club, where the main aim of many blokes who go there is to swap some saliva with a member of the opposite sex!

The Northern Soul scene revolves around rare records and those same bits of vinyl were, and still are, big business. A frequently packed corner of the Casino was the so-called 'record bar', although officially no such thing existed. It was an area near the downstairs bar at the rear of the dancefloor that was home to record dealers both professional and amateur. Minutes after the Casino doors opened, sellers lugging record boxes would grab tables and chairs and set up shop. They ranged from teenagers with an armful of 'sounds' for sale to raise much-needed cash to businessmen with hundreds of British and American releases all individually priced and in neat cardboard sleeves.

A visit to the record bar became the traditional first stop for most Casino-goers to see what gems were on sale. If someone had stopped to add up the street value of all the rarities on offer at any one time, the total would have been simply phenomenal. From 50p bargains to £50 'monster' records, imported US labels and UK releases were snapped up throughout the night. Some of the more professional record sellers would have signs showing what currently hard-to-find items were currently in stock. In 1981 it was not uncommon for rare singles to sell for £20 or more – even £100-plus for an ultra-rare side. Indeed, Russ Winstanley had a £1,000 record in Frank Wilson's soul recording 'Do I Love You? (Indeed I Do)'. No other copy has ever surfaced and Russ eventually parted with it for £1,000 worth of records.

Hundreds of more reasonably priced singles were bought and sold in the opening hours of each all-nighter and it was possible to become so immersed in searching through the vast quantity of collectors' items that a fair chunk of the night could be spent in the record bar. Labels like Okeh, Action, Columbia, RCA, Stateside, Cameo Parkway and Mirwood were revered by Northern Soul fans and anything on the original label in good condition was sure to fetch a good price. Many a mortgage or bad debt was financed in this way! At the same time, more readily available Tamla Motown releases were always popular and many collectors made a career out of trying to compile complete sets of the great label and its American alter egos, Tamla, Motown, VIP, Soul, etc.

The money-spinning potential of the record bar did not escape the attentions of the ever-alert Casino management, who made an ill-fated attempt to cash in. A £5 charge was levied on anyone selling records, on the premise that the Casino was giving dealers an unbeatable forum from which to do business and therefore should be entitled to a piece of the action. The move, however, backfired and the dealers voted with their feet – right out of the door. Only the professional record sellers were prepared to fork out a fiver; others simply went elsewhere. The result was a half-deserted record bar and quite probably a spin-off blow to attendances. The management had found out the hard way that the free-for-all record bar was one of the club's attractions and within a few weeks they relented and removed the £5 charge.

Whichever way you looked at it, Wigan Casino and Northern Soul were part of a totally unpretentious, working-class scene. If you could dance, knew the music or just wanted to become part of the movement, you were in. It didn't matter what your profession was, or even if you had one. This was a no-nonsense dance scene and any so-called 'professional' people dressed down for the Casino.

A particularly refreshing aspect was that the Northern Soul scene created itself and its own idols. Records were judged solely on their own merits, not by who the artist was, and would have to be dropped or played to death based on audience reaction. There were no Radio 1-style play-lists, where a

UK Soul Magazine's Rhythm & Soul's Top 30 in 1966. How many future Northern Soul favourites can you spot?

HOT THIRTY

1 (—) I'M MISSING YOU . . LORETTA WILLIAMS
US: Jotis 471/UK: Atlantic 584032   US chart: —

2 (—) WORKING IN A COALMINE . . LEE DORSEY
US: Amy 958/UK: Stateside 528   US chart: 5

3 (—) SUNNY . . . . BOBBY HEBB
US: Philips 40365/UK: Phillips 1583   US chart: 3

4 (—) YOU CAN'T HURRY LOVE . THE SUPREMES
US: Motown 1097/UK: Tamla Motown 575   US chart: 2

5 (—) SUMMERTIME . . BILLY STEWART
US: Chess 1966/UK: Chess 8040   US chart: 7

6 (—) YOUR GOOD THING IS ABOUT TO END
                                 MABEL JOHN
US: Stax 192/UK: Atlantic 584022   US chart: 6

7 (—) WILLY NILLY . . . RUFUS THOMAS
US: Stax 173/UK: Atlantic 584028   US chart: —

8 (—) SPRING . . . BIRDLEGS & PAULINE
US: Vee Jay 510/UK: Sue 4014   US chart: —

9 (—) BEAUTY IS ONLY SKIN DEEP
                          THE TEMPTATIONS
US: Gordy 7055/UK: Tamla Motown 579   US chart: 1

10 (—) IT'S BEEN SUCH A LONG WAY HOME
                          GARNET MIMMS
US: Veep 1232/UK: United Artists 1147   US chart: —

11 (—) LAND OF A THOUSAND DANCES
                          WILSON PICKETT
US: Atlantic 2348/UK: Atlantic 584039   US chart: 1

12 (—) LET ME BE GOOD TO YOU . CARLA THOMAS
US: Stax 188/UK: Atlantic 584011   US chart: 14

13 (—) SOCK IT TO 'EM J. B. . . REX GARVIN
US: Like 301/UK: Atlantic 584029   US chart: —

14 (—) OPEN THE DOOR TO YOUR HEART
                          DARRELL BANKS
US: Revilot 201/UK: Stateside 536   US chart: 7

15 (—) WANG DANG DOODLE . . KOKO TAYLOR
US: Checker 1135/UK: Chess 8035   US chart: 4

16 (—) I WANT TO BE WITH YOU DEE DEE WARWICK
US: Mercury 72584/UK: Mercury 937   US chart: 20

17 (—) LITTLE DARLING . . MARVIN GAYE
US: Tamla 54138/UK: Tamla Motown 574   US chart: 11

18 (—) HEADLINE NEWS . . EDWIN STARR
US: Ric-Tic 114/UK: Polydor 56717   US chart: —

19 (—) CAN'T SATISFY THE IMPRESSIONS
US: ABC Paramount 10831/UK: HMV 1545   US chart: 13

20 (—) REACH OUT I'LL BE THERE THE FOUR TOPS
US: Motown 1098/UK: Tamla Motown 579   US chart: 3

21 (—) TRAINS AND BOATS AND PLANES
                          DIONNE WARWICK
US: Scepter 12153/UK: Pye 25378   US chart: 49

22 (—) AIN'T NOBODY HOME . . HOWARD TATE
US: Verve 10420/UK: Verve 541   US chart: 15

23 (—) YOU GOT TOO MUCH GOING FOR YOU
                          JIMMY BEAUMONT
US: Bang 525/UK: London 10059   US chart: —

24 (—) LOVE IS A HURTIN' THING . LOU RAWLS
US: Capitol 5709/UK: Capitol 15466   US chart: 5

25 (—) BABY CAKES . . LORETTA WILLIAMS
US: Jotis 471/UK: Atlantic 584032   US chart: —

26 (—) JUST WALK IN MY SHOES . GLADYS KNIGHT
US: Soul 35023/UK: Tamla Motown 578   US chart: —

27 (—) SAID I WASN'T GONNA TELL NOBODY
                          SAM & DAVE
US: Stax 198/UK: Atlantic 584047   US chart: 18

28 (—) MAKE ME BELONG TO YOU BARBARA LEWIS
US: Atlantic 2346/UK: Atlantic 584037   US chart: 36

29 (—) I'LL GUESS I'LL ALWAYS LOVE YOU
                          ISLEY BROS.
US: Tamla 54135/UK: Tamla Motown 572   US chart: 31

30 (—) BLOWIN' IN THE WIND . STEVIE WONDER
US: Tamla 54136/UK: Tamla Motown 570   US chart: 1

The first column figure indicates the position the record was voted by readers and the second column shows the last edition's positioning. The US and UK labels and numbers are indicated below the title together with the highest number that the record reached in BILLBOARD's R & B chart at press time.

narrow selection of sounds was played over and over again. Soul fans did not like to be brainwashed into liking something. Perfectly good records sank without trace and resurfaced to great popularity years later, and the odd awful sound became inexplicably huge. The whole business was extremely unpredictable. With no 'hyping' of records and DJs unlikely to be influenced by any particular record company (for the simple reason that the label probably went bust a decade or more ago), the next £100 'monster' discovery was just as likely to come from a Bradford junk shop or a boxful of deletions from the States as from a record list.

An eight-hour Casino marathon was nothing if not sheer escapism. Time seemed to stand still as you were immersed in non-stop soul music. It was easy to forget that the outside world and all its problems existed when you were on the seething dancefloor at 5am, being totally caught up in a storming record, whether you were hearing it for the first time or it was already one of your all-time favourites.

Sometimes it would start snowing or begin to freeze and become treacherous outside, but even those with the longest journeys home would laugh through the windows. That was a problem for the morning; the night was for dancing.

In summer, the first indications that the night was drawing to a close would be when the first rays of sunlight started to creep through the upstairs windows. Gradually the dancefloors would start to thin out and the queue for the tea bar would grow as dancers waited to have a last brew before setting off home. The toilets would become unusually busy as soul fans trekked in for a quick wash and a last change of clothes.

Whatever respite there had been from the stifling heat as tiredness crept in and some soul fans departed early would be removed at 7am when Mr M's played its last record and hundreds of people would march downstairs into the Casino. Once again it would be standing room only as the last hour of the all-nighter dawned.

And still the beat went on. As 8am approached, it was time to locate your holdall and retrieve your coat from the cloakroom.

The famous 'Three before Eight' (Jimmy Radcliffe's 'Long After Tonight is All Over', Tobi Legend's 'Time will Pass You By' and Dean Parrish's 'I'm on My Way') gave an emotional lift to the end of the night. A steady handclap would punctuate each record and by the time Dean Parrish found his way on to the turntable there would often be the steady chant of 'More, more, more.' The final record and the turning on of the lights were inevitably met with a standing ovation as soul fans showed their appreciation of the night's entertainment. This finale usually merely whetted your appetite for the following week.

Getting out of the club was sometimes as slow as getting in, as weary soul fans crowded towards the exit doors and prepared to brave whatever the morning threw at them. Emerging from the cauldron of the Casino into the chill of a winter's morning and finding your car under 6 inches of snow was an experience to be missed. The sharp morning air in the still-dark outside world would come as something of an unpleasant jolt back into reality. In summer it would be the first blast of daylight as you stepped, blinking, into Station Road. Very rarely would there be more than a token police presence to watch over the soul fans as they made their way back to cars, buses, coaches, rented vans, minibuses, motorbikes, scooters and trains.

Others in less of a rush to get home would hang around chatting, saying goodbye to friends for another week or month, or would set off for a warming cup of tea. This was most easily found at Wigan Baths, only 200 yards or so away. Early-morning swimmers queuing for the international pool would suddenly find themselves surrounded by hordes of drawn, subdued soul fans. A small admission fee would get you into the café, which quickly became packed, and sometimes uniformed or plain-clothes police would come along to boost the numbers.

Other Casino-goers would brave a dip in the pool or have a refreshing shower before starting the long journey home. For those who still hadn't had enough, there was always Mr M's! For some time, it would reopen fairly soon after 8am to provide refuge for soul fans who had a while to wait for their bus or

⭐ WIGAN CASINO ⭐ ALL~NIGHTER

VISIT THE HEART OF SOUL
Every Sat.Night/Sun. Morning 12-30 a.m. - 8a.m.

FEATURING THE COUNTRY'S NO. 1 SOUL SPINNERS
RUSS WINSTANLEY & RICHARD SEARLING
PLUS TOP REGULAR GUEST D.J.s JOHN VINCENT, KEITH MINSHULL,
MARTYN ELLIS, ALAN RHODES, DAVE EVISON ETC. (FEATURING TWO
FLOORS WITH STEVE WHITTLE, ALAN, KENNY & BILLY PAUL IN
MR. M's PLAYING THE OLDIES)
NORTHERN SOUL NIGHTS EVERY WEDNESDAY (7.30—11 p.m.) and
FRIDAY (7.30—12 Midnight)
—FEATURING RUSS & RICHARD (NO MEMBERSHIP REQUIRED)

SAT/SUN SEPTEMBER 27th 12.30am–10am.

☆ 2ND ANNIVERSARY ALLNIGHTER ☆

Featuring Russ & Richard plus many Top Guest D.J.'s
100's Prizes To Be Given Away – Records, Cassette Players etc.
Final of our £100 Dance Competition
Every person will receive 'Special Edition' 2nd Anniversary Badge FREE
TICKETS £2 each + SAE (MEMBERS ONLY)
Don't Miss Out!! (Limited Quantity).

KEEP THE FAITH * **'HEART OF SOUL'** * **'NIGHT OWL'** Badges available 60p each
plus SAE
Car Stickers available, 30p each plus S.A.E. Also original 'Allnighter' Posters
approx 20in. x 30in. in 4 colours 50p each plus large S.A.E.

*TO JOIN OUR CLUB (FREE MEMBERSHIP) SEND FORM BELOW TO ARRIVE AT LEAST 48
HOURS BEFORE YOU DO.*

*WIGAN CASINO SOUL CLUB.
STATION ROAD, WIGAN
WN1 1YQ, LANCASHIRE
W.C.S.C. APPLICATION-
FORM FOR MEMBERSHIP...*

I (name) _
of (address) _
_ _
*DO APPLY FOR MEMBERSHIP TO WIGAN CASINO SOUL CLUB. I AM OVER 18 YEARS
OF AGE AND AGREE TO ABIDE BY THE RULES OF THE CLUB*

(P.S. Don't forget Beachcomber Soul Snack Bar open from 12 midnight to 2 a.m. and 6 a.m. — 10 a.m. for breakfasts (adj. Casino entrance)

train home (being Sunday service, it could be an hour or two). Of course, there would be the obligatory Northern Soul thumping away in the background (or more like the foreground). The Beachcomber café under the Casino also provided the same service at different times. For many people, however, eight hours of soul music inside the heat of the Casino was enough for one night and a breath of fresh air was a blessed relief.

The Casino's two large car parks would quickly empty and the drivers who weren't quick enough off the mark would be nabbed by the newly arrived car-park staff and asked to pay an overnight parking fee. Uncannily, within thirty minutes or so of the all-nighter finishing, hundreds of soul fans had melted away and Wigan folk came out for their Sunday-morning constitutionals untroubled by the Casino clientele.

Only six days to go to the next Saturday nighter …

2

They're Talking About Me

After DJing virtually alone for the first six months, apart from breaks for Ian Fishwick, Russ decided to bring in some more support. That came in the shape of budding young DJ Kev Roberts, who stayed at the Casino for a couple of years until business commitments took over.

Martyn Ellis became the regular oldies DJ and there were guest spots by Ian Levine, Colin Curtis, Frank (Ian Dewhurst), John Vincent and Steve Russell. Another DJ rapidly gaining a reputation at the Va-Va Club in Bolton was Richard Searling. He joined the Casino and was to become Russ's right-hand man and provide some wonderful soul records that helped keep Wigan at the top.

Brian Rigby and Alan Cain spun the sounds in the Beachcomber, and when Mr M's came into being after the first anniversary, the DJ line-up was Steve Whittle, Kenny Spence, Billy Paul and Alan Cain. There was no venue in the country which could boast such a solid collection of Northern Soul DJs and the Casino went from strength to strength.

In the second year Alan Rhodes, Dave Evison and Keith Minshull joined the roster. Alan Rhodes was replaced by Soul Sam and Pat Brady. Brian Rae also became a firm favourite with the Wigan crowd.

The enterprising Russ Winstanley was running his own record stall at the Casino but saw there was a gap in the market for Casino badges. Sew-on badges had become popular at other clubs, notably the Torch, and were to sell by the tens of thousands after Russ decided to market them. The first Casino badges cost 33p and retailed at 50p. Russ was well rewarded, as the ever-shrewd Gerry Marshall stepped in and bought the badges sideline from him. Some of the 'special' badges produced for the anniversary all-nighters became sought-after collectors' items and the mainstream badges were sold not only at the Casino but at record shops across the North-West, which were by then starting to stock Northern Soul imports.

The Northern Soul scene, pre-Wigan, had been very much an underground phenomenon. It had thousands of devotees up and down the country, quietly enjoying 'their' music in less-celebrated clubs than the Casino, swapping records and addresses with fellow soul fans and loving the exclusivity of it all.

That was to change as news of the Casino Club's contributions to youth entertainment started to reach the media and record companies. By the first anniversary of the all-nighters, the Casino was packing in the punters in such great numbers that its sister club in the Station Road complex, Mr M's, had to be opened to cater for the overflow from the main hall.

The reputations of the DJs, in particular Russ Winstanley and Richard Searling, were escalating and the all-nighters were playing, for many people's money, the rarest and best-quality Northern Soul sounds anywhere in the UK. Some of the records the DJs dusted off and turned into 'monsters' were so rare that record company bosses often could not remember buying up the original record labels or had mislaid the master tapes. Even so, London-based record scouts, sensing the whiff of easy money, started to get excited about the Northern Soul gems that might be lurking in their basements.

The Northern scene record hunters were turning up totally obscure American singles, little-known B-sides, unknown British releases and stunning album tracks with great regularity. The soul devotee with time and money on his hands had literally a decade's output of soul material to explore on second-hand stalls, record lists and junk shops for that elusive Northern gem.

Once played by a Casino DJ, a quality discovery could quickly attain cult status. After several months of playing to appreciative audiences, the value of a 50p discovery could easily leap hundredfold and everyone else in the country would be eagerly chasing copies. The climate was ripe for enterprising record company bosses to step in and re-release, or issue officially for the first time, an in-demand Casino sound that had already proved a hit on the dancefloor.

The music policy at the Casino was no accident. Every week the DJs would get together and discuss the latest rare sounds, play a few and decide which ones to unveil to the soul-hungry crowd.

According to Russ: 'We concentrated on certain records so that by the end of the night we could "break" perhaps three records and the next week we would stick with those again and introduce another four. I didn't mind lending the other DJs some of my own discoveries if they were screaming for them. The same record would be played perhaps three or four times a night and, if it took off, we were away.'

Such was the case with R Dean Taylor's 'There's a Ghost in My House'. This classic track, which eventually soared to number three in the UK pop charts, was originally on a mid-priced Motown album, *Gotta See Jane*. The white Motown singer had chart success with 'Gotta See Jane' and 'Indiana Wants Me'. But buried away at track three on the album and up to then unreleased as a single was 'Ghost in My House'. Right from the opening bars of the storming, handclapping song, Russ was hooked and knew it was tailor-made for the Northern scene: 'I remember putting it on the turntable and saying to myself, "Bloody hell." It had everything.' Other Northern Soul fans discovered its merits too and Russ admits that Ian Levine played it first at Blackpool Mecca, but, as he reflects: 'There's a big difference between playing it first and breaking it.'

The Casino decided to lean heavily on the 'Ghost' track and the response from the legions of dancers was astonishing. All over the country, record shops were doing brisk business in R Dean Taylor albums to soul fans. One can only assume that word got back to Tamla Motown bosses, who weren't mugs, and 'Ghost' was issued as a single in May 1974.

The B-side was the equally danceable 'Let's Go Somewhere', and with soul fans' support and radio airplay it catapulted into the charts. It stayed there twelve weeks and reached number three.

By this time, national newspapers were taking an interest in the strange disco which had no bar and was open *all night* playing obscure music. Wasn't everyone on drugs? The Casino was no longer a secret known only to its regulars and the local constabulary.

With record companies wondering, like Motown had before them, what other hidden Casino nuggets they had gathering dust in the vaults, the first guy to make the trip up north was Pye's Dave McAleer. Pye International had had a few British soul records, but more significantly they also held the rights to the American soul labels Roulette, Scepter and Wand, which were very collectable.

Dave was a soul fan and, realizing that his company could be sitting on a gold mine, he sought out Russ Winstanley. The resulting collaboration was the Pye Disco Demand label, which spawned a handful of hit singles and an album which also enjoyed healthy sales.

Casino dancers were already gyrating to the strains of Pye-owned records like the Casualeers' 'Dance, Dance, Dance', Frankie and the Classics' 'What Shall I Do?' and Al Wilson's 'Help Me'. The Pye man knew what soul fans liked and gave Russ an acetate (white label) of a studio track by a group calling themselves the Javells. It was a catchy, floating dancer called 'Goodbye Nothing to Say' and proved immensely popular with the Casino crowd.

Little did most people realize that the performers came not from Detroit or Chicago, but from a little closer to home – London. The guy behind the single was a white Jewish clothes seller called Steve Jameson. The Javells sounded better as a name – and in fact they were the black backing singers, brought in to give the record some 'soul' credibility. Steve wanted a performing name of his own, and, so the story goes, was inspired by a 'No Smoking' sign. So the group became Nosmo King and the Javells. The record, albeit of very dubious 'soul' origins, was a monster and on release in November 1974 reached number twenty-six in the pop charts.

Russ's answer to the soul purists is as follows: 'It broke very big within a few months. Listening to it, you couldn't tell if they were white or black. If the guy turns out to be white and someone is enjoying dancing to it, who are we to say we are not playing it?'

Steve's – sorry, Nosmo's – reward was brief fame and a spot on *Top of the Pops*. The Wigan Casino factor had again helped to establish a hit. But Northern Soul purists weren't happy – they felt they had been conned into liking a tailor-made record and couldn't associate with anything in the pop charts. I mean, fancy hearing a Wigan Casino sound on the radio after something like 'Chirpy Chirpy Cheep Cheep'! Not good for street cred.

That opinion wasn't helped by Pye's next Disco Demand release: Wayne Gibson's version of Mick Jagger and Keith Richards' 'Under My Thumb'. The Rolling Stones had always leaned towards black music and their tastes were often reflected in their music. Wayne – yes, he was white, again – had done a slightly speeded-up dance version of their song and no one made any pretence about the colour of his skin.

The song was rare, dancers at the Casino loved it and Pye and Russ saw another potential hit. McAleer leased the rights to the record from EMI and 'Under My Thumb' hit the pop charts in November 1974. Wayne was traced and signed up to appear on *Top of the Pops* with various Wigan Casino badges hastily stuck on to his shirt – another crafty marketing ploy.

Pye were delighted with the chart success of the Disco Demand series, but the best (or worst) was yet to come with the infamous 'Footsee'. In about September 1974, Russ had got his hands on a Roulette imported single called 'Footsee' by the Chosen Few. It was a pretty dire vocal dance song about an American baseball team, with an instrumental on the B-side. Russ played around with the instrumental, taped it, punctuated a few boring bits with sound effects and crowd noises –

handclaps, etc. – and played the re-recorded version at the all-nighter. Instrumentals were part and parcel of the Northern Soul scene and 'Footsee' seemed to slot in like the pure dance record it was.

Russ said: 'The people who went to the Casino absolutely loved it. They almost jumped off the balconies to dance to it. Of course, it was not a pure soul record – it was just a dance record. The only thing that came near to it in terms of popularity was "Afternoon of the Rhino" [Mike Post]. "Footsee" was an instrumental. I didn't see why I shouldn't play it. Does a black guy play an instrument better than a white guy, or more soulfully? Nobody knew what it was and I had a bit of fun putting it together.'

The slightly doctored version of the Roulette-issued original needed to be credited to someone, but the finished Pye Disco Demand release wasn't solely the work of the Chosen Few. How about Wigan's Chosen Few? It was the first time the Casino link had been spelled out on a release and certainly the first time any artist had used the name of the town.

One hurdle still to be overcome was the problem of the B-side. Russ and Dave McAleer plumped for 'Seven Days Too Long' by Chuck Wood. This was the genuine article – a thumping good rare soul sound that would be appreciated by soul fans long after 'Footsee' had been forgotten. It was chosen, as Russ puts it, to 'give the release some credibility' with soul fans and himself.

Russ designed the sleeve, based on a Casino badge, and wrote the sleeve notes. Pye Disco Demand had their biggest hit to date. 'Footsee' sold in vast quantities and reached number nine in the charts. It stayed in the Top Forty for eleven weeks from its release in January 1975. The signs were right straight from the start: the single received heavy airplay and was soon featured on Radio 1's *Round Table*. Russ remembers Emperor Rosko introducing the record as 'one of those Northern Soul things', and then playing Chuck Wood, either by design or by accident.

When it came to the offer of another spot on *Top of the Pops*, Pye were faced with the problem of producing an act to perform 'Footsee' for the cameras. The Casino agreed to choose a group of the best dancers from the 'early' Wednesday and Friday night sessions, which were regularly pulling in up to 900 youngsters, mainly from the Greater Manchester area.

The dancers made the trip down to London and turned in an athletic performance that astounded non-Casino goers and made Pan's People look like geriatric clog dancers. The nation's youth was hooked. What on earth was this Northern Soul stuff? (It was certainly nothing like 'Footsee'.) How did people learn to dance like that? Where could you hear this kind of music?

The whole Casino bandwagon was rolling on and gathering the speed that would ensure its lasting fame and its notoriety. Russ admits that, perhaps naively, he did not receive a penny for his efforts in getting Disco Demands into the pop charts: 'We had only been going just over a year. We wanted the prestige and the publicity. I was never paid a penny but I wanted to be seen as one of the people involved in the Casino. I ended up designing the sleeve and at the same time Pye said they would let me compile an album and put my name on it.'

After the astonishing success of 'Footsee', which sold more than 100,000 copies, and the album, which featured a picture of the Casino dancefloor on the cover, Russ was rewarded by Pye with twenty-five Barry White albums and a bottle of champagne. He declined the champagne.

The album, *Great Disco Demands*, featured the inevitable Wigan's Chosen Few, Javells and Wayne Gibson tracks. But it also had some class, and hitherto rare, soul in the shape of Chuck Wood, the Shirelles, Al Wilson, Frankie and the Classicals, etc.

Northern Soul – or what the pop-buying public sometimes mistakenly believed was Northern Soul – was by early 1975 *the* sound. It was suddenly hip to be associated with the music, and kids who had never been or even previously heard of Wigan Casino were packing holdalls and trudging off into the night to see what all the fuss was about.

All-nighters were soon springing up all over the country. Some were short-lived, some successful and others shut down by authorities that took a harder line than those in Wigan. Fans, who were too young or simply unable to go missing all night had to content themselves with the Casino's midweek 'early sessions' from 8pm to 11pm. Eventually there were soul nights at the Casino on Monday, Wednesday and Friday, together with the all-nighter on Saturday.

Record shops all over the North-West were selling Wigan Casino badges, freely obtainable Northern Soul records and the latest (and usually illegal) pressings of rare sounds. The years from 1975 to 1977 marked the heyday of the almighty stampede by record companies to find releasable Northern Soul material and a glut of singles and albums was released.

February 1975 saw the reissue of what was becoming an anthem at the all-nighters and the cornerstone of the 'Three Before Eight'. Dean Parrish's 'I'm on My Way' was a none-too-rare dancer which caught the imagination of many an all-nighter-goer.

Although white, Dean had a terrifically soulful voice and the atmosphere of the record, particularly when played to a packed dancefloor, was undeniable. As the last record at each Casino all-nighter, it had a cult following plus pop appeal. Russ, who traditionally played the final records of the night, recalled:

'Whenever I DJed anywhere I liked to finish off with a certain record rather than leave it to chance. I was playing "I'm on My Way" – it was just a good "last" record. It had an air of finishing to it but it wasn't particularly rare.' UK records issued Dean Parrish in this country and it crept into the charts at thirty-eight and stayed in for five weeks.

Another Casino-related 'hit' was by an already-established artist, Frankie Valli. Together with the Four Seasons, he cut 'The Night' with the Motown-linked label Mowest. Russ picked up on the recording and it went down a storm at the Casino. From the opening bass guitar riff to its storming conclusion, it was hugely popular.

As a result of the Northern Soul interest, Mowest issued 'The Night' and it stormed up the pop charts in April 1975 to number seven. Later another Four Seasons album track, 'I'm Gonna Change', would have a similar impact on the Casino dancefloor, confirming their cult following and the respect soul fans had for the group. (The American black soul group the Velours cut a version of 'I'm Gonna Change' which for many people's money was far inferior to Frankie's.

Seemingly Casino-backed records were never out of the UK Top Forty during 1975. As Russ says: 'It was a fabulous period. It was like every record company was saying to their people, "Get up the M6 and find out what's happening up there." We were playing the top type of contemporary music anywhere. We were really enjoying ourselves. It was the DJs who were dictating the records – nobody was telling us what to play.'

Casino manager Mike Walker was by now acting as 'agent' to his DJs, so anyone wanting to deal with Russ, Richard Searling and the others had to go through him. There were no more naive collaborations like the ones Russ had had with Pye.

The Casino bounced back with the ultimate marketing ploy: Wigan's Ovation. This infamous group was launched on the unsuspecting British public in March 1975, much to the chagrin of many Casino-goers, who felt the whole Northern Soul scene was being ridiculously exploited.

Wigan's Ovation were in fact a local white pop band called

Sparkle. John Smith from Spark Records – now a millionaire agent to many stars – came down from London and wondered how his company could cash in on the Casino boom. Sparkle, who often frequented the all-nighters but never played there, were doing Northern Soul stuff in their act at local clubs. One of the then popular songs at the Casino was 'Skiing in the Snow' by the Invitations, a fairly rare recording with a catchy chorus. The band did a version of this song for Russ, Mike Walker and John Smith in Mr M's one day, and the three men sensed the potential. They went down to London and recorded 'Skiing in the Snow' for Spark Records as Wigan's Ovation. On the B-side, in case anyone missed the Casino connection, was one they had written called 'Northern Soul Dancer'.

Russ said: 'They did some rehearsals and they didn't sound too bad. The lead singer, Jim McCluskey, had quite a soulful voice.'

Wigan's Ovation hit the big time and in March 1975 'Skiing in the Snow' was at number twelve in the pop charts. Self-respecting Northern Soul fans cringed at the sight of them on *Top of the Pops* with Bay City Rollers-type scarves, Wigan Casino badges and ridiculous high-waistband baggy trousers with 32-inch bottoms. (Of course, at that time everyone else was wearing ridiculous high-waistband baggy trousers as well!)

Russ countered: 'This group came along to us with an idea and all we got was a load of flak. We didn't get them together and we didn't push them into recording. They already existed as a group. A lot of people came here as a result of seeing them on *Top of the Pops*, but they were never on at the Casino and we would never have dreamt of putting them on.'

The group recorded two other hit singles with Spark: 'Per-son-ally', which reached number twenty-eight in June 1975, and 'Superlove', which made it only to number forty-one and disappeared after three weeks. Thankfully for many die-hard soul fans, that was the end of Wigan's Ovation's chart-busting exploits.

The Casino's marketing policy had alienated many all-nighter-goers, but had also brought in hundreds of new faces and generated masses of free publicity for the club. The all-nighters were becoming increasingly packed and special nights, such as anniversaries or those featuring live performers, often saw people still queuing to get in at 4am.

Month by month, master tapes were being dug out of the vaults and often given their first-ever UK release, or were re-released to satisfy Northern Soul fans' demands. The mid- to late 1970s saw a mad scramble in the music business to find releasable (and commercial) Northern Soul recordings. Many DJs were invited to compile various albums and/or work for both major and independent companies.

ABC put together *Out on the Streets Again*, featuring hard to find items like the Reflections' 'Like Adam and Eve' and Earl Jackson's 'Soul Self Satisfaction'. Grapevine, possibly the most collectable 'new' record label, was formed by John Anderson of Soul Bowl Records in King's Lynn, with Richard Searling playing a key role. The label produced several gems of the UK market, including Betty Boo's 'Say It Isn't So', and released three compilation albums, *Talk of the Grapevine, Sounds of the Grapevine* and *This is Northern Soul*.

Among the super-rare items finding their way on to vinyl at affordable prices were Eddie Parker's 'I'm Gone' and Tony Middleton's 'Paris Blues', as well as standard oldies like Richard Popcorn Wylie's 'Rosemary, What Happened?' and Maurice Chesnut's 'Too Darned Soulful'.

Destiny Records, formed by former Wigan Casino DJ Kev Roberts, weighed in with the compilation album *The Record Collector*, which, although it featured one or two good tracks, lost credibility by including cover versions of various Northern sounds it presumably couldn't get licensing rights to.

One source of in-demand Northern Soul sounds, although no albums appeared, was Black Magic. This label, set up by John Bratten, was part of Nottingham's Select-a-Disc and was one of the first specialist labels formed to cater for the Northern Soul boom. Black Magic provided Dobie Gray's 'Out on the Floor' on a UK 45 and saw it reach number forty-two in September 1975. The Sharonettes' 'Papa Ooh Mow Mow' made it to number twenty-six in April 1975 and in June a vocal/instrumental version of 'Going to a Go Go' reached number forty-six. Probably its best release, Bob Relf's 'Blowing My Mind to Pieces', didn't quite make it, and neither did Father's 'Angels with Bok to Bach', although both were appreciated by Northern fans.

Russ had a helping hand with Capitol Records' *Capitol Soul Casino*, a top-quality compilation of the label's monster sounds as played at the Casino and other venues. This monster included such nuggets as Nancy Wilson's 'End of Our Love', World Column's 'So is the Sun' and Bobby Parris's 'I Walked Away', which was both extremely elusive and 'red hot' at the all-nighters at the time.

After reissues and cover versions, the next logical step was always going to be 'tailor-made' Northern Soul records: that is, not genuine, obscure American recordings from years gone by but recently produced pop-oriented dance records using all the ingredients of the Northern Soul sound.

Among the first to see the market for tailor-mades was Blackpool Mecca DJ Ian Levine (see pages 61-7) – a million soul singles and many years spent listening to the Tamla Motown/Northern Soul sound had tuned him into what made a good soul record.

Other Casino/Northern Soul-related hits in those golden years of 1975 and 1976 included Betty Wright's 'Where is the Love?' (number twenty-five in April 1975), the Biddu Orchestra's 'Summer of 42' (number fourteen in August 1975), Al Wilson's 'The Snake' (number forty-one in August 1975), the Mike Post Coalition's 'Afternoon of the Rhino' (number forty-eight in August 1975), Tramps' 'Hold Back the Night' (number five in October 1975), Esther Phillips's 'What a Difference a Day Makes' (number six in October 1975), George Benson's 'Supership' (number thirty in October 1975), Rodger Collins's 'Sexy Sugar Plum' (number twenty-two in April 1976), and the Tavares' 'Heaven Must Be Missing an Angel' (number four in July 1976) and 'Don't Take Away the Music' (number four in October 1976).

There were also British releases for such sought-after items as Larry Williams's and Johnny Watson's 'Too Late', Derek and Ray Interplay's/Mike McDonald's 'God Knows', Julien Covey's 'A Little Bit Hurt' and Earl Wright's 'Thumb a Ride'.

Having watched all this going on around them, it was inevitable the Casino management would move towards signing their 'own' artists and eventually setting up the club's own record label.

3

Don't Bring Me Down

Someone once said that there's no such thing as bad publicity, and if that's the case, the Casino certainly got some good free 'plugs'. But its fame rapidly turned to notoriety and almost led to its downfall.

For the first couple of years of its existence, the Casino was hyped as *the* place for the younger generation to go. Of course, there was prejudice and misunderstanding, because many parents and middle-class, middle-aged people in authority could not comprehend why, or how, anyone would want to dance literally all night.

There had always been a certain stigma attached to Northern Soul all-nighters, and one or two of the Casino's predecessors had been shut down by the long arm of the law. It was often implied, and sometimes said openly, that youngsters needed stimulants to dance all night. This was, of course, a sweeping generalization and ignored the fact that young, healthy people caught up in the excitement and atmosphere of the music they loved needed nothing but their natural energy to get them through a sweaty six- or eight-hour all-nighter. That said, though, it cannot be denied that some people who attended the Casino took amphetamines – speed – to keep them going.

The rumour and innuendo surrounding the Casino were swept aside when a young woman who attended the all-nighters died from drug poisoning. The authors have decided to withhold her name to avoid causing the family distress. The *Wigan Observer* reported her death on 3 October 1975, under the headline 'All-nighter Drugs Probe'. It read:

> Allegations of drug trafficking at Wigan Casino's
> Saturday all-nighter are to be investigated by a coroner
> after the tragic death of a 20-year-old Wigan girl.
>
> The promise came from Cheshire coroner John
> Hibbert at the inquest on unemployed Miss X, of
> Worsley Mesnes, held in Warrington last Friday. Mr
> Hibbert said: 'From what I have heard about the Casino
> in Wigan, I think this place needs a bit of investigation. I
> will make my own inquiries about the Casino. I want to
> find out for myself.'
>
> Miss X was found dead in bed at a house in Widnes on
> 19 May. Dr J Benstead, pathologist, said the cause of
> death was morphine poisoning.
>
> Mr X said his daughter used to go to Wigan Casino
> despite his objections. Sometimes she would come home
> at 10am in the morning, and even in the afternoon. She
> also loved to travel to places in Manchester.
>
> Det Const A E Sharples, of Cheshire Constabulary,
> drugs squad, said of the Casino that it was believed
> drugs were passed there and there had been numerous
> arrests. But more information with regard to the Casino
> could only come from the drugs squad operating in that
> particular area, he said.
>
> Mrs X, the girl's mother, said at the inquest that she
> wrote to the Chief Constable in Manchester just after
> her daughter had been taken into hospital with a drugs
> overdose in 1974.
>
> She reported in her letter what was allegedly going on
> at the Casino and the Chief Constable replied that he
> was looking into it. But the Casino was still open, she
> said.

In the same issue of the *Wigan Observer* was a letter from an
anxious mother who objected to the way the paper was
'glamourizing' the Casino. She wrote:

Recently I have been disgusted at the articles on the soul nights at the Wigan Casino. These articles have been written in such a manner as to imply to teenagers that they are missing the major event of the year, instead of conveying the much truer picture to them and their parents of the likelihood of being introduced to the drugs scene.

I recently have become involved via a very close friend in the horrors of this practice, he having lost approximately three stones in weight in as many months. My fear of his involvement was heightened only recently by the tragic death of a young girl barely out of her teens after a trip to the Casino.

Only this evening were we treated to a nauseating article in your newspaper. I read that the people at the Casino are angry at the imputations of drug taking at their club. I'll bet they aren't as angry as the friends and relatives of the teenagers involved in drug taking.

I only hope that the police inquiries being started can manage to get this and other places like it closed down – and that a paper with the reputation of the *Wigan Observer* will play its part by giving publicity to the dangers our children are exposed to.

The *Wigan Observer* defended its stance in its 'Opinion' column in the same issue. It said:

One reader has criticized the *Wigan Observer* for giving publicity to a Northern Soul event at Wigan's Casino Club. Just one reader is enough for us to show our concern. But there is something to be said against the argument that the all-night sessions at Wigan Casino should be closed down.

The prime function of a local newspaper is to react to local events. Therefore we could hardly be expected to ignore an event which attracted 1,500 people to Wigan from all over England. The event would have been held with 1,500 people present whether the event had been mentioned in the *Wigan Observer* or not.

Chief criticism of the Northern Soul all-nighters is that they are a vehicle for drug taking. Certainly few, if any, people can dance non-stop for eight hours without pep pills of some form or another. The almost complete absence of police prosecutions for drug taking inside the Casino suggests that a serious problem does not exist.

The *Wigan Observer* must and does come out strongly against drug taking. But is it conceivable that every week hundreds of young people travel up to 200 miles to Wigan Casino just to get pep pills that must surely be available on their own doorsteps?

Observers of the Casino scene from this newspaper describe the all-nighters as noisy, repetitive, sweaty, sexless and sometimes boring affairs. Why, people don't even dance together because of the dangers of physical damage from outflung legs and arms.

It is asking too much to expect everybody to applaud Northern Soul with all its trimmings. Its devotees seem generally to keep themselves to themselves and when all is over return peacefully whence they came, which is more than can be said for some soccer and rugby fans.

One crime is that some youngsters have mistaken the pay box at Wigan Baths for the north-west railway station. There's many a drunk who lost his way too.

Rumour and accusations continued and a fortnight later the *Wigan Observer* reported that the local MP, Alan Fitch, had stepped in. Under the headline 'Drugs Storm – Wigan MP Acts', the newspaper reported:

Wigan MP Alan Fitch is seeking talks with police officers over alleged drug trafficking at Wigan Casino's all-nighter soul sessions.

The move follows Mr Fitch's meeting last Friday evening with two constituents who wish to remain anonymous, but who, he says, provided him with evidence about drug activity at the nightspot.

Mr Fitch says he was given examples of Wigan people who were now suffering as a result of drug taking at the all-nighter. He said there was a case of one youth 17½ years old who started taking drugs seven months ago and he has since lost over three and a half stones in weight.

He said: 'There are other examples and obviously this is a very serious business indeed. I have no doubt that there is a need for some action to be taken.

'Now I am seeking urgent discussions with Chief Supt Norman Lindsay of Wigan police about the situation. Depending on the outcome of these talks I will decide whether or not to get in touch with the Home Office.

'I will want to know what the police view is on this matter and see what they know about it.'

Mr Fitch said evidence of alleged drug activity was not easy to come by as people weren't very inclined to speak.

He said: 'The evidence I have is limited but it's disturbing. I feel it's sufficient to warrant me taking the matter further.'

Last week Wolverhampton MP Nick Budgen called for an inquiry after a mother had complained to him that her daughter had taken drugs at the all-nighter.

Wherever large crowds of young people gather it is likely that some drugs will be found. The Casino was attracting well over 1,500 people every week and it was inevitable that some of the dancers would have drugs.

Where illegal drugs were recovered, they were usually amphetamines in the form of powder or 'pep pills'. Because of the Northern Soul tradition that dancers would carry holdalls containing changes of clothes, the Casino management were placed in an impossible position. It would clearly have been impractical to search everyone and their belongings – not to say extremely unpopular with the dancers – so stopping drugs entering the club was no simple matter.

Staff were constantly on the look-out for suspicious activity and many of the regulars recognized that the club they loved was in jeopardy and that any further drug incidents could prove the final nail in the Casino's coffin. Toilets were regularly checked by the 'bouncers' and it was by no means a rare occurrence to be sitting in a cubicle to find the door suddenly being kicked open by a doorman.

Many youngsters who dabbled in drugs discovered a new vocabulary in the Casino. 'Gear' was the street name for drugs and users knew the most common forms of speed (amphetamine sulphate) by pseudonyms: black bombers, green and clears, chalkies, blueys, and dexys.

To the untrained eye it could be difficult to spot those who used amphetamines. But generally, speed users were wide-eyed, hyperactive and tireless, dancing for hours on end, talking animatedly and frantically chewing gum.

One former regular said: 'It was fairly easy to get hold of gear at the Casino. There was always something going around if you wanted it. But you never got guys coming up to you offering you stuff and it was all very discreet. I think a lot of people who wanted it bought their stuff before they even set off for the all-nighters. There were never any hard drugs like heroin and cocaine going around, and of course ecstasy wasn't even heard of back then.

We used to do speed because it was part of the Northern Soul experience and just something that you did to keep you going all night. I knew guys who wouldn't dream of going to an all-nighter without taking speed, but there were lots of people who never bothered, or tried it and didn't like it. It didn't matter as long as you were into the scene.'

Russ accepts that some drugs were smuggled into the Casino, but says the scale of the problem was overestimated by people who wanted to close the all-nighters down: 'If you believed everything you read it was horrendous. Even my mum and dad used to wonder about the place until I invited them in. You could go into any pub and club in the country and find drugs and the Casino was no worse. When the Casino was going it used to be convenient for anyone found with drugs to say, "I got them at the Casino." It saved them naming the real person who had sold them the stuff.'

The Casino did, however, become tainted with a drugs reputation and drugs squad officers and uniformed police were regular visitors. The Casino management used to make a room available to visiting officers and cooperated totally.

Dancers got used to being searched occasionally in the freezing car parks at some unearthly hour, having their cars turned inside out or being whisked off to the nearby police station to give a urine sample. Russ recalls that some Smarties police found in his van were taken away for analysis. For a time the mere presence of a Wigan Casino sticker on a young person's car was seen by some police officers to indicate that international drug dealers were on board.

Eventually the Wigan MP and chief of police went to the Casino to see for themselves. According to Russ: 'They asked where they could go and we said they could go anywhere and speak to whoever they wanted. I think they were expecting to see people lying in corners with syringes in their arms. When they came back Mr Fitch said he couldn't believe the atmosphere – he said it was fabulous that all these people were here just to dance.'

Then the Casino got some good news after months of uncertainty. On 28 November 1975 the *Wigan Observer* reported 'All-nighter cleared of Drug Guilt'.

> The drug scene at the Casino in Wigan is not as bad as it has been suggested, it is revealed in a report to Wigan MP Mr Alan Fitch from the Greater Manchester Assistant Chief Constable in charge of crime, Frederick Richards.
>
> Mr Richards said his officers were satisfied that the majority of young people who go to the club aren't interested in drugs. They go for the music and the dancing.

He said: 'The facts speak for themselves. Since the all-nighters began in September 1973, only eight people have been successfully prosecuted for possessing controlled drugs on the premises. Over 200 people have been searched for drugs in the vicinity of the club and there have been about 90 court appearances. These people have been found near the railway station in Wigan and the surrounding streets.

There is obviously a problem which we could loosely associate with the Casino but there is no evidence that the Casino is responsible. The Casino management cannot be blamed.

So there it was. There was a certain amount of drug abuse, but it was not on the massive scale that some suggested and the Casino management could not be held responsible. And compared to today's widespread abuse of the dance drug Ecstasy and related deaths, whatever problems the Casino had now appear relatively minor.

That is not to say that speed was not taken by many Casino regulars, or to deny that many people got into trouble with the law, their families or their employers as a result of taking illegal substances at the weekly all-nighters.

The simple fact is that the club could not possibly have remained open if police believed there was a serious problem. The all-nighters carried on for eight years before they were brought to an end, not through police objections but through local planners and a lease agreement. But that's another story ...

4

I'm Where It's At

Anyone who wasn't already aware of the Wigan Casino phenomenon was aroused from their slumbers in the winter of 1977, when the story invaded the country's living rooms via a Granada TV documentary.

In keeping with the entire history of the all-nighters, the thirty-minute *This England* programme inevitably caused controversy among the club's regulars, staff and ordinary Wiganers. It was hugely popular with some viewers, indifferently received by most and slammed by many locals and those associated with the Northern Soul scene. In any event, it went on to be one of the most watched programmes of the year, strongly challenging the viewing figures of established favourites like *Coronation Street* and *The Generation Game*. More than 20 million people tuned in, making it the third most watched programme of the year.

The documentary had been heavily plugged in advance and became an eagerly awaited item among the army of soul fans and not a few parents. So, on December 12 1977, at 8.30pm, the country settled down in front of their TVs to watch the finished product. It started promisingly enough, with shots of Wigan's past and present industry, glowing furnaces and canals interspersed with a slow-motion shot of the Casino's packed dancefloor and a lad performing a fast, multi-revolution spin. In the background the MVPs' 'Turning My Heartbeat Up' came crashing in and more pictures of Wigan's past, Wigan Pier service station and an advert for Uncle Joe's Mint Balls let the

WIGAN CASINO SOUL CLUB
presents Sat./Sun. Morn.   *12-30 a.m. - 10 a.m.*
SEPTEMBER 24th, 1977
We're Four years old ! ! !

4th Anniversary 1973 - 1977
ALLNIGHTER

featuring Russ & Richard plus lots of guest spinners
on TWO FLOORS

---

*Every person will receive a Special Souvenir Embroidered
Badge FREE of Charge*

100's Anniversary presents to be given away !

Final of the Annual £100 Dancing Competition !

Many well known 'Soul' people will
be with us to help celebrate Four   **N⁰   0833**
unbelievable soul-packed years.

TICKETS £3 EACH

audience know that this programme was, indeed, about Wigan.

Bolton's Dave Withers was chosen as spokesman for the legions of male Casino-goers. He summed up the feelings of many when he told the interviewer about how he was met with bemusement whenever he told people he went to Wigan Casino on a Saturday night. People didn't understand, thought it was a gambling den, and were even more puzzled when they discovered it had no licensed bar and Dave didn't go there to pick up girls. He spoke eloquently of the special place the Casino held in the hearts of its regulars.

'To get enjoyment out of life in their teens and early twenties, people have to build more or less an alternative society just to enjoy themselves,' said Dave. 'It brightens up the lives of the people who go. I suppose the world even now isn't ready for people doing anything too extraordinary. You have got to fit in. If you go up to Wigan on a Saturday night, stop there all night and come home about one o'clock the next day, people think you are crazy, or there's something going on. They're not willing to accept it and say, "They probably have a very good time doing that." '

One of the most enduring images of the documentary featured a wonderful aerial shot of the Casino's packed dancefloor to the strains of Judy Street's 'What?' Some great dance sequences, including atmospheric slow-motion shots, made it immensely watchable. Richard Popcorn Wylie's 'Rosemary, What Happened?' Rain's 'Out of My Mind' and the Lovelites' 'Get It Off My Conscience' were also featured to a greater or lesser extent.

But the mistake the programme-makers made in many people's minds was linking the Casino too closely with Wigan's past. There were scenes of derelict and crumbling areas, dirty-faced street urchins from decades gone by, and grimy miners. In reality, the Casino phenomenon had little to do with Wigan. Only a small percentage of the crowd came from the immediate area and the all-nighter could have been situated in any North-West town. It just so happened that the Casino was the ideal venue – before that, Manchester and Stoke-on-Trent had hosted similar underground events.

With uncanny foresight, Dave Withers talked about the authorities who shut down all-nighters and the prospects after the Casino had gone. He said that people who didn't want all-nighters would probably welcome the Casino's demise, thinking they had 'cleared the city of a load of bums', but that councils did not realize they were affecting people's whole lives with a stroke of a pen.

'If Wigan shut down I wouldn't know what to do. It would be like instant nostalgia. That would be it. I would be thinking, "God, am I going to be looking back for the rest of my life?" I wouldn't really be able to cope with life, I would have to sort my life out again. I couldn't start going to normal clubs,' said Dave.

A female regular was filmed on the dancefloor and at work as the programme-makers attempted to show how her ordinary

WIGAN CASINO ALL~NIGHTER

VISIT THE HEART OF SOUL

Every Sat. Night/Sun Morning Midnight-8am

FEATURING THE COUNTRY'S NO. 1 SOUL SPINNERS

RUSS WINSTANLEY & RICHARD SEARLING

Plus Top regular Guest D.J.s KEITH MINSHULL, BRIAN RAE, SOUL SAM, PAT BRADY, DAVE EVISON etc. and other top guest soul spinners. (Featuring two floors with KENNY SPENCE, BRIAN, STUART & GAL in Mr. M's playing THE OLDIES) ● NORTHERN SOUL nights every Wednesday (7.30-11 p.m.) and Friday (7.30-11 p.m.) ● Featuring RUSS & STUART (NO MEMBERSHIP REQUIRED).

The Big One!

Friday/Saturday Morning   12 Midnight to 8a.m.

FEBRUARY 1st

"Come and listen to those memories"

4th ANNIVERSARY
OLDIES ALLNIGHTER

(would you believe it!)

8 NON-STOP HOURS OF OLDIES ON TWO FLOORS, FEATURING ALL THE TOP REGULAR OLDIES SUPER-SPINNERS, PLUS LOTS OF GUESTS.

100's SPECIAL BIRTHDAY PRESENTS TO BE GIVEN AWAY
PLUS EVERY PERSON WILL RECEIVE SPECIALLY EMBROIDERED ANNIVERSARY BADGE

FREE ON THE NIGHT!

ADVANCE TICKETS £3.50 each

(MEMBERS ONLY)
SEND P.O.'s ONLY and S.A.E.

Be early - Everyones Comin!

TO BECOME A MEMBER YOU MUST BE OVER 18
— MEMBERSHIP IS NOW 25p
Applications to arrive 48 hrs before you do.
Please send SAE

Wigan Casino Soul Club.
Station Road, Wigan,
WN1 1YQ. Lancashire
W.C.S.C. application
form for membership . . .

I (name)...

of (address) ....

....

Do apply for membership to Wigan Casino Soul Club. I am over 18 years of age and agree to abide by the rules of the Club.

existence was brightened up by the weekly Saturday night soul sessions. Asked what she would do after the Casino had gone, she replied: 'Life would be just a big bore, that's all there is to it. That's where all my mates are and I wouldn't have any way of getting in touch with them. If Wigan Casino finished I would either look for another all-nighter similar to it or I would just stop going out, I think. I would just stop in and deteriorate.'

Russ could see the direction the programme-makers were taking with the documentary, fell out with them and as a result was not featured in the finished version. His initial reservations proved right when it was broadcast. As he has said: 'I wasn't that struck on it. There were some good dancing shots but all the flashback stuff to old Wigan and the girl working in the launderette was a waste of fifteen minutes of it.'

The reaction to the Granada documentary was summed up for many by the *Wigan Observer*, which carried a story on 16 December 1977 under the headline 'Leave Us Alone Rap for TV':

> The message to Granada TV came over loud and clear from Wiganers this week: Leave our town alone unless you can paint a true picture.
>
> Following yet another programme – *Wigan Casino*, shown on Monday night – which concentrated yet again on the clogs and shawl image of the town, Wigan people voiced their protests.
>
> For although the programme purported to be about the goings-on with the Casino's all-nighter soul club, it was interspersed with views of Wigan, mainly of what little derelict property there is left. Twenty-five people who work for the education department in Wigan Metro have signed a petition in a bid to get a truer picture of Wigan shown.
>
> The petition has been sent to Granada with the comment: 'While we are proud of Wigan's industrial past, we fail to see what relevance it has to present-day Wigan Casino.' A Metro spokesman said: 'We have had

a lot of calls from people complaining about the image of Wigan shown on the programme, but it was nothing to do with the council.'

Mr Alan Wright, researcher for the programme at Manchester, said that by Tuesday afternoon there had been only two adverse calls. Ex-Wiganers have also voiced their protests. Mrs Susan Molyneux, now living in Kelso, Scotland, wrote to the *Observer*: 'I just feel downright ashamed about ITV's biased one-sided view of a wonderful town. How did they find such shots of parts of the town? Can they not show the good with the bad? (And there's not much bad now?)'

Mr Wright said that members of the all-nighter had phoned to congratulate him on their capturing on film the atmosphere of the soul sessions. Viewers were allowed a peep at what draws thousands of young people to Wigan Casino every Saturday for a marathon dance. And the attraction, contrary to public opinion, it seems, is not drugs.

Mr Wright said: 'There might have been a drug problem at the all-nighter two years ago when a small minority took or peddled soft drugs, but you would get that kind of thing in any nightclub. I think the problems at the Casino have been solved partly by a clamp-down by police but also by the members themselves, who are so afraid that the Casino might be closed because of drugs that they themselves act as the best possible police force.'

5

Competition Ain't Nothin'

Lots of other all-nighters came and went during Wigan Casino's reign, but for many soul fans the Casino's main rival was the legendary Highland Room at Blackpool Mecca in Central Drive. Sadly, the vast building now stands empty, but like the Casino its memory lives on.

Although never an all-night venue, it was undoubtedly one of the key places of the 1970s. And the chief architect of the Mecca sound was one of the most influential and controversial Northern Soul DJs of all time, Ian Levine.

Ian's ear for music led him eventually, as already mentioned, into a highly successful record-producing career, at first producing 'tailor-made' Northern Soul records using his own black American artists and more recently helping to give Take That and Bad Boys Inc. commercial dance records. Between 1971 and 1979, Levine reigned supreme at the Mecca complex in Blackpool.

From teenage spinner to record producer on both sides of the Atlantic, he attracted admirers and critics in equal numbers. He was a guest DJ at one of the first Wigan all-nighters, but he later became the target of ill-tempered campaigns to remove him. So how did a Blackpool-born soul collector provoke such passionate reactions?

Ian Levine started DJing at the Highland Room at Blackpool Mecca in 1971 at the tender age of seventeen. His record collection was already phenomenal and his reputation for unearthing records and his taste in music meant that he rapidly

BLACKPOOL MECCA— Highland Room

EVERY SATURDAY — 7·30 p.m. — 2·00 a.m.
The place that's established beyond any shadow of doubt as the Country's No. 1 Soul Place.

DJs

COLIN CURTIS

IAN LEVINE

Once again unfortunately we dare not list any of the records we play. That contemptible underhand French individual from California keeps on trying to find out what we're playing here at the Mecca and keeps on sending those illegal pressings over, so if you find we're keeping a few of our new sounds rather hushed up, this is the reason why. As soon as this evil person stops his antics we will print a list of our top records once again.

There is definitely NOWHERE whatsoever to compare to the Mecca. We have records nobody else in the Country has. It's the place to be every Saturday

SOLID SOUL SENSATIONS

gained a good reputation. He and his colleagues Tony Jebb, Les Cockell, Keith Minshull and Colin Curtis ensured that Blackpool Mecca was a force to be reckoned with. Ian guested at the Torch all-nighters in Stoke, but it was the Saturday night sessions in Blackpool that made his name.

The soul gatherings there were during 'normal' disco hours, unlike the all-nighters, and finished at 2am. Smart dress was needed as the club was part of the Mecca complex, which housed a cabaret and pop club. The Highland Room was a neat, oblong-shaped room dominated by a large dancefloor, and hundreds of soul followers crammed in as its popularity grew. Punters came from all over the country, often en route to an all-nighter. So, when Wigan Casino opened its all-nighters, the Highland Room became the 'starting point' for a weekend of soul for many devotees. Hundreds of smartly dressed dancers would lug their holdalls containing several changes of clothes along. At 2am, or earlier, stage two of the weekend would come into operation with the hour-long trip to Wigan. Often there would be a Sunday all-dayer somewhere in the North-West and if they could still stand, soul addicts could leave Wigan at 8am for there.

As an endurance test it was unparalleled: Blackpool Mecca, Saturday, 9pm to 1am; Wigan Casino, Sunday, 2am to 8am; and, say, the Ritz all-dayer in Manchester, Sunday 12 noon to 10pm – just about twenty-four hours of almost non-stop soul music, sometimes accomplished without the benefit of, or desire for, any sleep whatsoever. Work on a Monday morning was not a welcome prospect!

The Blackpool nights were particularly attractive to

Russ (*far left*) is awarded DJ of the Year's silver disc in 1974. With him are his girlfriend Doreen, Frank Elson of *Blues and Soul* (*right*) and Dave McAleer of the Pye Disco label (*far right*).

Staff of Casino Classics.

Casino owner Gerry Marshall, assistant manager Harry Green and a familiar face at the cash desk, Hilda Woods. (*Dave Motler*)

Manager Mike Walker draws the raffle at the club's first anniversary celebrations. An off-duty Wigan policeman (*far left*) and DJs Ian Dewhurst and Martyn Ellis look on.

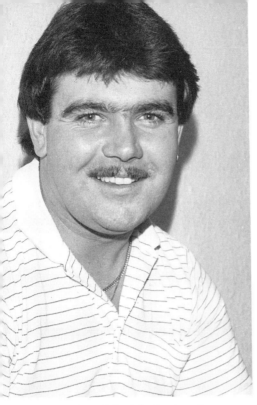

Casino DJs (*clockwise, from top left*) Chris King, Keith Minshull,
Steve Whittle and Richard Searling.

The Casino (*above*) and its sister club, Mr M's, in its early cabaret days (*below*). (*Wigan Observer*)

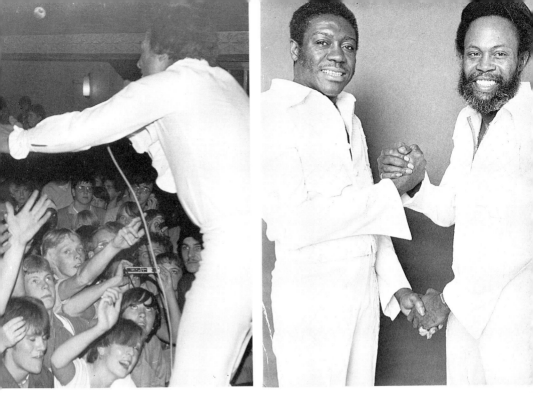

Casino star Tommy Hunt, on stage at the second anniversary all-nighter, Sam and Dave (*Barry Plummer*) and (*below*) Kevin Rowland and Dexy's Midnight Runners.

Soul singer Gloria Jones and Marc Bolan, with their baby Rolan
(*Press Association*), Edwin Starr and (*below*) Motown favourites
the Temptations.

Singers (*clockwise, from top left*) James Brown, Major Lance, Marc Almond and Martha Reeves.

Motown singers the Marvelettes (*above*) and the Supremes (*below*).

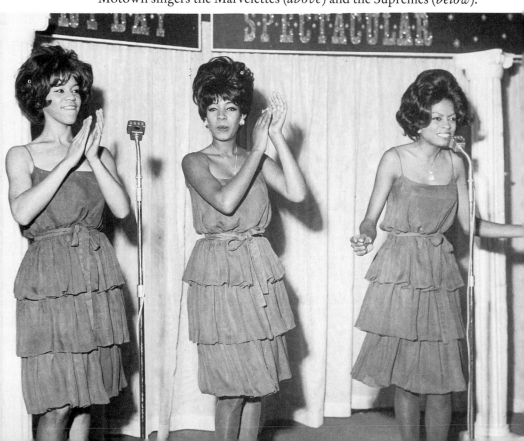

non-car-owning soul fans who fancied a trip to Wigan afterwards. Several coach firms operated free transport to and from the Mecca from towns across the North-West. The Wigan coach driver who earlier that evening had arrived in Blackpool with a half-empty coach was often astonished to find himself taking twice as many home with him. Passengers with unfamiliar Scots and Geordie accents would swear blind they had been on the outward journey.

That is not to say that the Mecca did not have its own appeal. The music was deliberately different to that played at Wigan and the rivalry was quite intense, but, on reflection, it was healthy for the soul scene.

If one club 'broke' a stunning record, the other's nose was out of joint. As Wigan leaned more towards oldies and the 1960s soul sound, Ian steered the Mecca towards something more modern. That made the Wigan/Blackpool split even greater and started great debates in soul circles about whether the discofied 1970s stuff which eventually dominated the Highland Room constituted Northern Soul.

Ian has said: 'The Casino was a wonderful place, but the longer it went on the worse the music became. They started to move towards white pop stompers and it moved away from the traditional Northern beat. It was a shame. That was one reason why at the Mecca we moved towards 70s disco records. They went to one extreme and we went to the other. Records like 'The Larue' had that good clean stomping sound but some of the stuff they played at Wigan had nothing to do with Northern Soul.'

Ian's ear for a tune led him to make records rather than merely discover them. In 1975 he went to New York at the invitation of the Exciters, Herb and Brenda Rooney, whom he had met when they were on a British tour. Ian signed them up for a recording session in New York and he wrote and produced the songs.

As he recalled at the time: 'I'd never written anything before. It all seemed to come instinctively from playing soul records for years.'

BLACKPOOL
MECCA

"Tiffanys", Central Drive, Blackpool
THE COUNTRY'S NUMBER ONE NORTHERN SOUL HAVEN

SPECIAL FIFTH ANNIVERSARY CHRISTMAS AND NEW YEAR CELEBRATIONS

On Boxing Day, Friday 26th December 1975, to commemorate Five Years of Northern Soul at Blackpool Mecca

THE BIGGEST SOUL EVENT OF THE CENTURY
FIFTH ANNIVERSARY ALL-DAYER

12.00 noon — 12.00 midnight   Admission: £1.00

**DJ's: IAN LEVINE, COLIN CURTIS
KEV ROBERTS, LES COKELL**

Plus lots and lots of special surprises to be revealed.

We are proud indeed to be the longest running major Soul venue in the country, and prouder still that we were able to put on such an event to coincide with our Fifth Anniversary. Don't miss it. It's gonna be a sell out.

PLUS!!!!

EVERY SATURDAY AS ALWAYS
THE HIGHLAND ROOM
8.00pm — 2.00am

**DJ's: IAN LEVINE
COLIN CURTIS**

Still going strong after five years. The country's Number One Soul Venue.

Wednesday 24th December
XMAS EVE
in the HIGHLAND ROOM
8.00pm — 2.00am

Have a brilliant Xmas with all the very best sounds around that you'll hear anywhere in the world on Xmas Eve.

DJ's: IAN LEVINE
COLIN CURTIS

Wednesday 31st December
NEW YEAR'S EVE
in the HIGHLAND ROOM
8.00pm — 2.00am

The best night of the year at the Mecca. See everybody there to hear the first solid Soul sensations to be played in 1976 with IAN LEVINE and COLIN CURTIS

To all the thousands of people who've kept the Highland Room 'Number One' over the last five years. A Very Merry Xmas and Happy New Year.

His first production, 'Reaching for the Best', got into the Top Fifty in Britain in 1975, through 20th Century Records.

He collected together a pool of artists and released to considerable success the Northern Soul-influenced 'Your Magic Put a Spell on Me' (L J Johnson), 'Weak Spot' (Evelyn Thomas), 'Heading Down Fool's Road' (Carol Woods), '24 Hours a Day' (Barbara Pennington) and a host of others.

Of course, his own productions featured heavily on his play-list at the Mecca and this caused some resentment among soul fans. The purists objected to what they saw as tailor-made records by a white producer being thrust at them. Ian admits on reflection that his productions, and the birth of the Casino Classics record label, contributed to an element of overkill with mass-produced Northern Soul-style records.

The Mecca started to lean more towards 1970s records as the Casino stuck to its predominantly 1960s play-list, which led eventually to a distinct split in the audiences the two attracted. But even though the rivalry between fans of the two venues sometimes became heated, Russ insists there was never any bad blood between the DJs of Blackpool and Wigan: 'Our rivalry was a bit like that of Manchester United and Liverpool. We got on great with Ian Levine and Colin Curtis. It was the different factions of the fans that seemed to be at loggerheads at times. I never had any problems with either of them. They both did guest spots at Wigan and they certainly wanted to do more, but I didn't think it would be right if they did. With hindsight I think I was right, because a lot of the 70s stuff they were playing wasn't particularly rare and was southern stuff rather than good solid Northern Soul. Now when people come up to me and request records, all they want to hear is 60s stuff. No one wants to hear "Shake and Bump" and stuff like that.'

One time Russ will admit to feeling pleased at 'beating' the Mecca is when he started to play Yvonne Baker's 'You Didn't Say a Word'. Levine thought he had everything on the Cameo Parkway label and disputed whether the Yvonne Baker side – now a Northern Soul anthem – even existed.

Russ recalls how Levine's sidekick Les Cokell was dispatched to the stage at the Cat's Whiskers in Burnley to check on the record as Russ played it. The Wigan DJs were amused to see the consternation caused in the Mecca camp as the news was relayed to them.

One man who confirms the Casino's superiority over the Mecca as a venue is former Casino DJ Pat Brady, now a Leeds-based record dealer. He DJed at the all-nighters on alternate weeks for the last three years of the Casino's life. According to Pat: 'I can remember thinking as a kid when I first started to go to Wigan that the Mecca was better. There was a time when the music at Wigan was crap. But the Mecca could never touch Wigan for atmosphere. They played some great stuff at the Mecca, but you could hear the same record at Wigan and it sounded totally different because of the atmosphere and the venue. Historically as a dance venue Wigan was far more important than the Mecca.'

By the latter part of the 1970s, with the Mecca concentrating on New York disco music, funk and later jazz/funk, Ian proudly proclaimed: 'Northern Soul is dead.' His critics became more and more vocal. A 'Levine Must Go' campaign was launched, with a petition and badges circulating at soul events at which he appeared. At combined Northern Soul/Modern Soul events, Ian stuck firmly to New York disco and modern disco

---

Nº 1868

WIGAN CASINO SOUL CLUB
presents
Sat./Sun. Morn   12 midnight to 8 a.m.
SEPTEMBER 22nd
"WE'RE SIX UNBELIEVABLE YEARS OLD"

Nº 1868

1973 to 1979   **6th ANNIVERSARY**   1973 to 1979
ALLNIGHTER

Featuring RUSS and RICHARD plus all our regulars, plus lots of GUEST JOCKS
OLDIES ALL-NIGHT IN M's
with KENNY, BRIAN, STUART and GAL

100's Fantastic presents to be given away — Radio's,
Watches, Cassette Recorders etc., etc.
+ including MUSIC CENTRE worth over £300
GRAND FINAL of our ANNUAL DANCE COMPETITION
1st Prize £100   2nd Prize £75   3rd Prize £25
DON'T FORGET TO ENTER
Every person will receive special FREE SPECIALLY
WOVEN SOUVENIR BADGE FOR OUR 6th ANNIVERSARY
Lots of Soul Personalities promise to be with us —
DON'T MISS OUT!!!
TICKETS £3.50 each (Members only) tickets limited

PLEASE RETAIN THIS PORTION
OF YOUR TICKET FOR SPECIAL
6th ANNIVERSARY DRAW at 4 am

sounds, alienating the fans who had once worshipped him.

Ian had grander ideas than simply DJing and went on to produce High Energy records when he was DJ at the top London gay club Heaven. But a decade later the pull of Northern Soul proved irresistible. In 1989 he set up his own Motorcity records and signed a host of former Tamla Motown recording stars, including the Supremes, Kim Weston, the Elgins … and Frances Nero.

She was only about fourteen when she recorded 'Keep on Loving Me', which had a cult following on the northern scene. Ian got Frances, by now working in a Detroit minicab office, to go back into the studios for the first time in more than twenty years to record an album. She redid 'Keep on Lovin Me' under Ian's guidance and provided the label with its first British Top Twenty hit in the spring of 1991 with 'Footsteps Following Me'.

Ian said: 'The idea with Motorcity records was to get Motown artists under one roof again. Northern Soul was based around the Motown sound and when Motown dried up, everybody started looking around for Motown-style stuff on other labels. Northern Soul owes a lot to Motown and we are now putting back something that we have taken out.'

Ian even showed his renewed interest in the Northern scene by making a guest appearance at a Northern event for the first time in twelve years – at the Torbay Weekender in April 1991.

Wasn't he the man who said Northern Soul was dead?

Ian's reply: 'It was dead, but musically I don't think anything better has ever replaced it.'

Part II

The Sounds

6

Nothing Can Compare to You

In this chapter, Russ Winstanley first lists his favourite fifty Wigan Casino discoveries and then, in his own words, tells the story of how some of these records – which pre-Casino were long-forgotten and often on doomed labels – came to be part of the Northern Soul legend.

1. 'Do I Love You?' Frank Wilson (Soul/Motown)

The ultimate Northern Soul sound as well as the world's rarest record. The last record to be played at the all-nighters, at 9.10 am on 7 December 1981.

2. **'Time Will Pass You By'**   Tobi Legend   (Mala)

The words and voice say everything. Took ages to break but well worth it.

3. 'You Don't Love Me' Epitome of Sound (Sandbag)
I originally covered it as Moses Smith. The epitome of Northern Soul.

4. 'Double Cookin'' Checkerboard Squares (Villa)
Could have been written for Wigan. Initially covered and pressed as 'Strings a Go Go' by Bob Wilson.

5. 'You Didn't Say a Word' Yvonne Baker (Cameo Parkway)
Everybody asked me for the 'James Bond theme'. Ian Levine said it didn't exist. Superb.

6. 'Woman, Love Thief' Stemmons Express (Wand)
Haunting and very moody. All-nighter sound at its best.

7. 'I Have Faith in You' Detroit Symphony (Gordy)
Incredible instrumental of Edwin Starr's song. It just builds and builds. Great feel-good factor.

8. 'My Sugar Baby' Connie Clark (Joker)
Unusual tempo. Written by Frank Wilson (enough said).

9. 'I Go to Pieces' Gerri Grainger (Bell)
Became the 'Fourth before Eight'. Those words, that voice. Written by the guys who wrote 'I Will Survive' for Gloria Gaynor.

10. 'I'm Gonna Change' The Four Seasons (Philips album track)
That beginning, that tempo, that voice. I love Mr Valli, 'The Night', 'You're Gonna Hurt Yourself', 'You're Ready Now'.

11. 'You're the Life' Mary Wilson (Motown)
A 70s sensation covered as Candy Staton. Fabulous floater.

12. 'Afternoon of the Rhino' Mike Post Coalition (Warner Bros)
The searing strings, 600mph sound. Led to the fable of 'lemmings' jumping off the balcony to dance to it. A sixty-six-piece orchestra conducted by twenty-one-year-old Mike Post in 1969.

13. 'I Can't Help Lovin' You' Paul Anka (RCA)
Ultimate white soul dancer covered as Johnny Caswell. Shouldn't have covered it. Nobody believed me when I told the truth!

14. 'New York in the Dark' Ad Libs (Eskee)
Grittier than the Wigan Rugby League team. Recorded in 1965, massive in 1978. Outstanding production from the New York city boys.

15. 'If You Ever Walk Out of My Life' Dena Barnes (Inferno)
Another mid-tempo monster dissected by a wondrous vocal.

16. 'You Got Me Where You Want Me' Larry Santos (Evolution)
Different sound and tempo from this self-penned Latin vocalist. Became a firm favourite.

17. 'Loving is Really My Game' Brainstorm (Tabu)
A 70s stomper missed by the Mecca. Outstanding arrangement.

18. 'Night Owl' Bobby Parris (Cameo)
Summed up our scene in words and music. A 1963 stomper. The name of my house!

19. 'Dance Dance Dance' Casualeers (Roulette)
The lyrics, tempo and excitement. An early Wigan discovery.

20. 'If This is Love' Eddie Spencer (Uptown)
Certain sounds make the hairs on your neck stand up. This was one of them. Amazing.

21. 'I'm Not Strong Enough' Four Perfections (Jo-Dee)
Another 1973 discovery. Wistful vocals over intriguing arrangement.

22. 'Put Your Loving Arms Around Me' The Sherrys (JJ Records)
My first discovery, prior to the Casino. The first record to be played at the Heart of Soul at 2am on 23 September 1973. A 1966 Phillybuster. Helped to start a legend.

23. 'I'm on My Way' Dean Parrish (Laurie)
Evokes so many memories. The final record at every nighter, except the last one. Always makes me feel sad. Dean Parrish was actually an Italian guy called Phillipe Anastasie – sorry!

24. 'If You Want to Go Back Baby' Jean Cairn (Philly)
Who said I only played 60s stompers? Another 1970s gem of a floater.

25. 'You Don't Know Where Your Interest Lies' Dana Valery (Columbia)
Out and out 60s stomper! Written by Paul Simon.

26. 'Love Music' Sergio Mendez (Bell)
Unusual slow- to mid-tempo Latin-influenced tune. Sergio never credited the girl singer so I called her Sue Hunt!

27. 'Too Much of a Good Thing' Ambassadors (Peevee)
That dirty sax and brass intro says it all. Dancers delight. Voluptuous vocals.

28. 'Long After Tonight is All Over' Jimmy Radcliffe (Musicor)
Loved this Bacharach and David classic for years. Delighted it was accepted in the infamous 'Three Before Eight'. What an intro!

29. 'You Didn't Have to Leave' The Illusions (Lamon)
Dripping with soul. Unbeatable emotion in both the voices and the instruments. You can smell the Casino.

30. 'Jumping at the Go Go' Detroit Sound (Wyncote)
Get out the talc for the spins. Frantic Philly production proved to be a dancers' delight.

31. 'Better Late Than Never' Diane Ducane (Con)
Had to laugh when one review said she had never been further south than Watford! Beautiful black lady born in Jamaica, living in New York. Mid-tempo magic.

32. 'What?' Judy Street (Strider)
A non-pretentious stomper conceived on America's West Coast. I chose it for the Wigan Casino TV documentary in 1977.

33. 'God Knows' Mike McDonald (RCA)
What an emotional song and performance. A record that I never tire of.

34. 'Do What You Wanna Do?'   Michelles   (Wand)
Reminded me of the sounds and reasons why I got into the scene. Essential excitement that rocked the sprung dancefloor.

35. 'I'll Always Need You'   Dean Courtney   (RCA)
Instant smash with dancers and DJs alike. Should really be higher than number thirty-five!

36. 'Pain in My Heart'   The Poppies   (Epic)
The real title is 'The Love We Knew' but I covered it as 'Pain in My Heart' and it stuck. A real girl's song. One of my first discoveries. Lead singer was Dorothy Moore of Misty Blue fame. Unforgettable.

37. 'Love Bandit'   Keenya Collins   (Barnabus)
Spoken into. Sugar and spice content. Nice change from pounding stompers.

38. 'Help Me to Find Myself'   Outsiders   (UA)
I covered it as the Detroit Shakers. Did shake the building to the foundations. Ideal break for handclapping. Monster.

39. 'You Keep My Temperature Rising'   L J Johnson   (Philips)
Great 70s production originally covered as Barnaby Bye. Never uncovered until today!

40. 'Help Me'   Al Wilson   (Wand)
Another all-nighter anthem. Perfect beat. Released on Pye Disco Demand.

41. 'Baby Hit and Run' Contours (Motown)
'Why are you playing this? You can buy it for 60p.'
'Because it's bloody brilliant.'
It still is. A hidden gem from 1974.

42. 'Broadway' Renee Prior (Spring)
Another 70s stomper. Well worth watching out for.

43. 'Music with Soul' Pallbearers (Musicor)
The Wigan sound in just two and a half minutes. It has got everything except much soul!

44. 'My Place' Devastating Affair (Mowest)
Same label as the superb 'Night' by Frankie Valli. Wonderful voices but difficult tempo.

45. 'Tears' Lee Roye (MCA)
What an opening. What a memory jerker. Found it in a box under my bed!

46. 'L-O-V-E' Leon Thomas (CR)
Took five years to break as it was so unusual. Still a sought-after rarity.

47. 'Can't Get Along without You' Dutch Robinson (Sceptre)
Singalong sensation. Great crossover 60s/70s tune. Luckily never pressed.

48. 'It Didn't Take Much' Percy Wiggins (RCA)
Massive floor filler that became in demand everywhere.

49. 'All of a Sudden'   Jeanette Williams   (Backbeat)

A powerful Texas tune that I was delighted to reactivate. Equally impressive is her other monster, 'Something Good's Got a Hold on Me'. Cream of the crop!

50. 'I Love Music'   The O'Jays   (Philly)

Yep, surprise, surprise, I first played this in Station Road. The O'Jays have always been my favourite group since the Neptune classics 'Looky Looky' and 'Deeper in Love'.

There will always be debates about who first played, discovered or 'broke' which sounds. Again, an argument will reign about who supplied what to whom. If that's the case, then my Uncle George, who has lived in Fort Lauderdale since 1967, must surely get the credit.

Soul Bowl's Jon Anderson must be the 'hidden phantom', guiding Richard Searling to play his gems. My uncle used to ship thousands of discs to me. Others came from Simon Soussan, many outlets in New York, Val Shively's in Philadelphia, 8 Miles Out in Detroit and many local trips to Global's warehouse in Manchester or Bostock's in Bradford.

Goldmine's Martin Koppel sent me lists from Canada and Balham's record corner came up with the occasional gem. All of my suppliers, including Manchester's Brian '45' Phillips, would regularly send certain titles with 'Gonna Be Massive' written on them! Supplying it and breaking it were as different as chalk and cheese. Usually your hunches paid off, but occasionally a record you felt must make it didn't and vice versa. I felt that people voted with their feet and attendance.

I wanted to please as many people as possible, not be the collectors' God and play brand-new sounds each week to a dismal dancefloor. I feel that I got the balance right, breaking some new gems, playing some classic oldies and resurrecting some forgotten tunes. This was instilled into the DJs and part of the reason I felt that Ian Levine and Soul Sam played more for themselves   than the people who paid their wages. From around 1979, some DJs' egos were becoming too inflated and politics started entering their play-lists.

Back to my fifty. I broke all of them at the Heart of Soul playing 90 per cent of them before anyone else. I was born within 2 miles of the Casino, have always lived within a couple of miles of the place, and will no doubt pop my clogs in similar proximity. My wife, Doreen, and my daughters, Dionne and Jodie, are all well versed in my last wishes. A certain four anthems are to be played at my funeral: 'Long After Tonight is All Over', Jimmy Radcliffe; 'Time Will Pass You By', Tobi Legend; 'I'm on My Way', Dean Parrish; and 'Do I Love You? (Indeed I Do)', Frank Wilson. As all soul lovers will know, the first three songs were played each week from 1976 as the last three records before 8am to finish the nighters.

When released on RK Records (RK 1004), the 'Three before Eight' maxi single initially charted at number forty-three before Gallup excluded it from the listings as it had only sold regionally. In the first week it sold 25,000 copies. The A-side, Tobi Legend, was radio Luxembourg's 'Twin Spin' record of the week.

Over a quarter of a million sales later, it still sold in the 'wrong' shops (ie not chart return ones) and never charted!

These three essential tracks are again available on the first *Wigan Casino Story* CD by Goldmine Records that I helped to compile in 1994 with ex-Casino DJ Kev Roberts. I believe that the maxi single will also be available in 1996.

If I'm just remembered for founding the nighters and the 'Three before Eight' tracks, I'll be extremely happy. I include Frank Wilson's 'Do I Love You?' as, again, it epitomizes the outstanding music and memories created in the centre of Wigan in the 1970s. Being an avid black music collector since my early teens in the mid-1960s, 'Do I Love You?' was the only piece of vinyl on Motown's subsidiary label Soul that no one had ever seen or heard of. I had to satisfy my curiosity!

Through my contacts in the States, the disc was 'borrowed' from Motown's vaults and was soon winging its way to my turntables. It had been dormant since its conception on 23

November 1965 and I could hardly believe my eyes when I opened the parcel. I became even more excited when I saw that it was also written by Frank Wilson, who had penned and produced many Motown hits. There it was at last, 5-35019 'promotional', 'not for sale'. It had been stored between Earl Van Dyke's 'The Flick' and 'Keep on Loving Me' by Frances Nero.

With the perspiration building up, I carefully wiped the black vinyl and checked some slight damage to the edge of the disc. I slowly and carefully lowered the arm on to the grooves and prayed that it wouldn't be a ballad! I needn't have worried. That irresistible Motown dance beat soon broke through, an incredible opening of piano, strings and vocals to die for. I was astounded. Could this be the best Motown/Northern Soul sound ever? It soon proved to be so in many people's eyes. Being the world's worst dancer, I just jumped up and down, shouting: 'Yes, Yes!' It was January 1978 and as Doreen brought in my cuppa, she enthused: 'You're right, it's incredible!' Hands now trembling, we played it again and again.

'Are we exaggerating or is it really so superb?'

'No, it definitely is!'

'As usual, I couldn't wait to get to the Casino to break it. There was a problem, though. What if there were more copies knocking about? Around 500 demo discs were usually circulated to radio stations in the 1960s. What if, initially, I cover up the label and artist and say it's by another artist? This was the usual way of keeping a sound to yourself for a while, yet I was one of the few DJs who disliked doing so. I felt it was cheating.

One of my favourite singers was a guy called Eddie Foster, who had a monster sound called 'I Never Knew' and the vocals were similar. So that was it. 'Do I Love You?' by Eddie Foster was born. One final stroke, though. As I was convinced of its rarity, I had the song transferred to an acetate copy, generally called an Emi disc. Each week we programmed a number of new tunes to try to break, but I knew this was special. I played 'Do I Love You?' first and introduced it as a new track by Eddie

Foster. It was an immediate success and dancers and collectors hurried to the stage with cries of: 'What the hell is that? It's a monster!'

There had only been such quick recognition for a few records and these had generally become classics. Discoveries falling into this category were 'Afternoon of the Rhino', Mike Post Coalition; 'I'll Always Need You', Dean Courtney; 'I'm Gonna Change', Frankie Valli and the Four Seasons; and Checkerboard Squares', 'Double Cookin' ', covered as 'Strings a Go Go'.

'Do I Love You?' was soon acknowledged as one of the best Wigan discoveries and a phone call to Frank Wilson established that it was probably the world's only one-off. After having the initial 500 advance copies pressed, he decided he hadn't the time to promote it and so 499 copies were destroyed.

'There's only one copy left and that's in Motown's vaults,' said a bemused Frank.

'Oh, no, it isn't,' I thought to myself.

Due to its phenomenal popularity, I finally uncovered it in mid-1979 and Motown in Britain released it in November 1979 (TMG 1170). Being 'too Northern' for radio, it never reached the charts and British demos are still selling for around £30. In 1980 I was finally tempted to part with it (should never have done so), for £1,000 worth of swaps. It has only swapped hands once since ... for £5,000. Ah, well.

As I had made the rules of playing the three anthems before eight o'clock, I played them on the last night of the Casino. After playing them again, no one wanted to leave, so I played 'Do I Love You?' a few times until it finally sunk in at 9.10am – one of the saddest and most moving moments of my life.

Now you know how important these four musical gems are to me, and hundreds of thousands of other soul lovers, you will realize why I've chosen them for my own emotional farewell.

Now, David Nowell takes a look at his Top Twenty Wigan Sounds –

not necessarily all Wigan discoveries, just sounds that evoke memories of the greatest club in history!

1. 'Countdown (Here I Come)' The Tempos (Canterbury)
The essential 100mph dancer. Massive production, soaring strings, piercing vocals. Defies anyone to stand still, even at 7am. Funny how it sounds faster and faster the older I get.

2. 'The Drifter' Ray Pollard (United Artists)
The 'ender' record to end all enders. Will forever conjure up the image of Brian Rae finishing his spot at the oldies all-nighters. More of a beat ballad than a dancer, but for me it just leapt out amid the normally frantic Wigan sounds. Dripping with emotion and a voice second to none.

3. 'What Kind of Lady?' Dee Dee Sharpe (Gamble)
Great intro and stunning vocals. Classic Mr M's sound. The first time I heard this the hairs on the back of my neck stood on end. How on earth could someone who could belt out a song like this fail to become a superstar?

4. 'I'm Not Strong Enough' Four Perfections (Jo-Dee)
Another Mr M's stunner. Great horns, chugging rhythm and slightly sparse arrangement give this a real gritty feel.

5. 'You Didn't Say a Word' Yvonne Baker (Cameo Parkway)
A true classic that has stood the test of time. One of the most distinctive sounds ever, and one that I find even appeals to many non-soul fans. Put it on the turntable, hear the intro and you are back on the floor at the Casino.

6. 'Don't Depend on Me' Fantastic Johnny C (Phil LA)
One of the many 'reactivated' oldies that became massive at the Casino. Mid-tempo, smooth but tailor-made for handclaps. A feel-good record.

7. 'If That's What You Wanted' Frankie Beverley (Sassy)
The best-ever intro to a Northern Soul side? Sharp horns, rolling drums and Frankie's shouted vocals combine to bring this timeless stomper crashing in. Superbly atmospheric.

8. 'A Little Togetherness' Younghearts (Canterbury)
From the same stable as the Tempos. No wonder the label went bust – how could they afford to keep throwing in a thirty-six-piece orchestra on every track without having any hits? Another uplifting stomper with so much to listen for in the arrangement.

9. 'House for Sale' Millie Jackson (Spring)
Untypical mid-tempo Wigan sound from the mid-70s. First played as an album track. If Millie's brilliant voice doesn't get you, the words will. I remember getting a letter published in *Blues and Soul* in which I praised this record. Within a couple of weeks it was released as a single. Can I claim some credit? Until someone refutes it, that's my story and I'm sticking to it!

10. 'Hung Up on Your Love' The Montclairs (Contempo)
Perfect slab of 70s soul. Unique intro, brisk pace, wonderful harmonies. Begs to be listened to right to the final second.

11. 'Stick by Me, Baby' Salvadors (Wise World)
Played so often at Wigan (or even overplayed) that it was only in later years that I realized just how good it was. Epitomizes Northern Soul from the sax intro to the usual dancefloor applause as it fades out.

12. 'I'm Gone' Eddie Parker (Sha-rae)
Gutsy, aggressive vocals, sexist lyrics, powerful stuff. No one screams a song quite like Mr Parker. Much better than 'Love You, Baby', his other biggie.

13. 'How Long?' J J Barnes (Contempo)
I always thought this soulful version of the Ace pop song was under-rated and was pleased when Dave Evison revived it at the Casino and it became massive. A slice of smooth 70s soul.

14. 'I Really Love You'   The Tomangoes   (Washpan)

Pure power, a sparse production and a lead vocal that demands to be listened to. A Northern Soul gem. Raw and satisfying.

15. 'I Wanna Give You Tomorrow'   Benny Troy   (Delite)

Another 70s floater with the feel-good factor. Totally ignored these days but deserved a new airing.

16. 'You're Gonna Make Me Love You'   Sandi Sheldon (Okeh)

What kind of Top Twenty would it be without this one? Always a guaranteed floor packer, bringing back memories of a hundred sweaty, noisy nights and mornings.

17. 'Main String'   Oscar Perry   (Peritone)

A Mecca sound or a Wigan sound? Who cares. Associated just as much with the Casino as with the Highland Room via the Wigan oldies nights. Another 70s glider which always provided a welcome contrast to the 60s-dominated play-lists at Wigan.

18. 'Meet Me Half Way'   Lillie Bryant   (Tayster)

It's 3am at an oldies all-nighter in 1980 and I'm standing smoking a cadged cigarette while leaning against a wall near the stage. Me and Nick from Blackburn are chatting away ten to the dozen and this record comes on. The atmosphere is buzzing and everything feels right. I decide not to dance, but continue talking while letting the music wash over me. Lillie Bryant, wow, forgotten how good this was! What were we talking about? God knows, but I only have to hear this sound and I'm back there.

19. 'It Really Hurts Me, Girl'   Carstairs   (Red Coach)

All right, another Mecca sound really, but it got a thousand plays at the Casino and became a massive oldie. Uniquely manages to combine real soulfulness with a more modern feel. Handclaps compulsory.

20. 'So is the Sun'   The World Column   (Tower)

The supreme stomper. A massive, aggressive, masculine sound which rocked the all-nighters twenty years ago. Rarely played these days for some strange reason.

As the Casino's success grew and all-nighters became more and more packed, the club started to add to its regular Saturday events by holding specialist Friday all-nighters.

So started the highly successful oldies all-nighters, which began in February 1976 and took place every month. For a scene that is based on 'old' records of up to thirty years old, it will seem bizarre to outsiders to talk about 'old' and 'new' Northern Soul sounds. But oldies were regarded as well-known sides played in the past at the Casino or the Torch and the Twisted Wheel before it. 'New' sounds, even though they might be of the same vintage, were recent discoveries which were being 'broken' by a DJ and gathering cult status in venues around the country.

Dave Evison is thought by many to be the thinking man's oldies DJ, and is still very active on the Northern Soul scene today. The son of a wealthy businessman and an ex-pupil of the prestigious Millfield public school, Dave got into DJing by accident in Belfast during his army service in 1969. He was partial to the 1960s R and B band the Animals and through their music got to know and enjoy the real thing on Tamla Motown, Atlantic, Stax, etc.

In 1967 he started to frequent the Twisted Wheel in Manchester and, like hundreds of others, was hooked on the music. Surprisingly, unlike today's Northern Soul scene, much of it was new releases, as the American soul labels were in their heyday and churning out new products week by week.

After leaving the army, Dave turned his hand to more DJing, doing two spots at the Torch and enjoying the live acts by the likes of Major Lance, and – wait for it – the Stylistics! Dave was working with Casino DJ Kev Roberts at the Top of the World in Stafford when Wigan first opened, and between them they managed to get him a spot at the Casino all-nighters, which had then been running about six months.

Dave recalled: 'Martyn Ellis was the only one playing oldies at the time. I concentrated on quality Northern Soul oldies, but I never paid more than £5 for a record. I was a dancer before I was a DJ and still am – I have never forgotten my roots. The most worrying moment for me was after I had played the last record at my first spot in Wigan. I jumped straight back on the dancefloor and everyone started clapping.'

His eye for reactivating oldies brought cult status and increased values to a warehouse full of sounds as diverse as Spyder Turner's 'I Can't Take It Any More', Millie Jackson's 'House for Sale', Benny Troy's 'I Want to Give You Tomorrow' and George Benson's 'On Broadway'.

The hard work that Dave and his fellow oldies DJs put in (he also did a spot in Mr M's) in promoting 'old' records with the Casino faithful led to the demand for the oldies all-nighters. These events were always packed to capacity and as the years went by many regulars opted for the once-a-month oldies nights rather than the weekly Saturday event. Attendance at the Saturday event immediately after the oldies was usually noticeably down.

Said Dave: 'It's ironic that we might have created the beginning of the end for the Saturday nights.'

At the risk of causing a rift between the authors, Dave Nowell's experiences bear out the view that for many the monthly oldies all-nighters became a focal point rather than the Saturday events.

Many people visited both, of course, but as the early 1980s arrived, along with unemployment for growing numbers of youngsters and family commitments for some soul fans, travelling up to Wigan every weekend became impossible. Once a month seemed to be the ideal, and the monthly oldies, with their always-familiar music, were convenient dates for the diary.

Russ, however, does not agree that the oldies events harmed the Saturday all-nighters: 'The attendance on the night after the oldies was down a lot, but only by the Casino's standards.

There were still more people than in your average nightclub. We decided that if people really enjoyed the Friday oldies all-nighters then we ought to give it them.'

The oldies nights, and occasional specialist nights, like the successful Tamla Motown Friday all-nighters, gave the Casino formidable pulling power. At its peak, the venue was running 'normal hours' discos on Monday, Wednesday and Friday, a monthly Friday oldies all-nighter and occasional specialist all-nighters, 'early' Saturday sessions and, of course, the weekly Saturday all-nighter. That was one hell of a week if you had the time and the money to do it all!

And now for Russ's outstanding oldies:

1. 'Can It Be Me?' Mel Williams (Modern)
Massive in 1973, loved everything about this stomper. Can picture the packed floor now!

2. 'Soul Self Satisfaction' Earl Jackson (ABC)
Summed up my philosophy – still does! Two and a half minutes of 1966 dynamite.

3. 'I Never Knew' Eddie Foster (In)
Again, memories of the first magical all-nighters. Tremendous.

4. 'Call Me Tomorrow' Major Harris (Okeh)
Floated to Wigan from the Mecca. One of the scene's favourite labels.

5. 'One Way Out' Martha Reeves (Motown)
When I told Martha how popular it was, she sang it without any backing live on stage – wonderful!

6. 'Queen of Fools' Barbara Mills (Hickory)
Echoes of my first visits to the Blackpool Mecca. Just haunting! Still as good.

7. 'Open the Door to My Heart'   Darrell Banks   (Revilot)
Coupled with another standard, 'Our Love is in the Pocket', this is what Northern Soul was named after.

8. 'You Gotta Pay Your Dues'   Drifters   (Atlantic)
Another mind-blowing intro, incredible vocals and pace. Simply superb.

9. 'Move on Up'   Curtis Mayfield   (Curtom)
Must have been heard by virtually everyone. Totally under-rated writer and vocalist. Triggers the feel-good factor again.

10. 'Friday Night'   Johnny Taylor   (Stax)
Another of the collectors' favourite labels. The adrenalin and the feeling of the oldies all-nighters come straight through.

11. 'Nothing Can Compare to You' Velvet Satins (General American)
Another early floor-filler. Released in my favourite year, 1966. Very few compare to this.

12. 'I Get the Sweetest Feeling'   Jackie Wilson   (Brunswick)
I just love his ultra-smooth voice. Such a shame he was unwell when appearing live. Check out 'Nothing But Blue Skies'. Soul Music with a capital 'S'.

13. 'Come on, Train'   Don Thomas   (Vee)
Dedicated to everyone from Manchester who never purchased a ticket and nipped off the train at Ince. Awesome!

14. 'Wade in the Water'   Ramsey Lewis   (Chess)
1973 in the Beachcomber and Mr M's DJs Alan Cain, Bri Rigby and Dave Swift.

15. 'Moody Woman'   Jerry Butler   (Mercury)
Motown to 'Moody Woman'. The classic start for many youngsters. Produced and written by Gamble and Huff. The voice himself, Jerry Butler.

16. 'My Weakness is You'   Edwin Starr   (Gordy)
Probably the scene's finest live act. So many gems. 'Back Street', 'SOS', 'Contact'. I remember how he sang over my 'Faith in You' backing track – a living legend.

17. 'What Kind of Lady?'   Dee Dee Sharpe   (Action)
Kenny Gamble's missus. This is what singing is all about. Dee Dee Sharpe Gamble also sings my favourite song in the world, 'Nobody Could Ever Take Your Place', on Philly International.

18. 'Be Young, Be Foolish, Be Happy'   Tams   (Stateside)
Anthem of the times. Happy-go-lucky song. Nostalgia rules.

19. *Motown Memories Album*   (Motown)
This album plus the silver *Chartbusters Volume 3* and a few bottles of cider used to get me into most parties in 1967! These were the little-known Tamla artists: 'I'll Always Love You', Detroit Spinners; 'Put Yourself in My Place', Elgins; 'I Want to Go Back There Again', Chris Clark; and 'Come and Get These Memories', Martha and the Vandellas are all featured. Wonderful!

20. 'Cook Jerk'   Supercharge   (Criminal)
Liverpool's finest with an awesome version. Told Andy Parker I'd feature it.

21. 'Next in Line'   Hoagy Lands   (Laurie)
One of the first rarities I knew of. Used to be taken to Wigan Rugby Club for Neil Swann to play. Absolutely outstanding cut.

22. 'I'm Coming Home in the Morning'   Lou Pride
(Suemi)
Stomper from Texas produced by Kenneth Smith. Summed up the night owls. Searing voice.

23. 'It Really Hurts Me, Girl'   Carstairs   (Red Coach)
Mecca monster. So much soul. Could play it for ever. Always made me and Richard laugh as we passed through Carstairs in Scotland.

24. 'Darkest Days' Jackie Lee (Mirwood)
Richard loved the label so much that he named his cat after it. Also had a daughter called Golden World. Sorry Carolyn, only joking! One of the first sounds to get me into the scene. One of the best.

25. 'Out on the Floor' Dobie Gray (Charger)
Must be in everybody's top thirty. The excitement, dancing and production. Tony Jebb sold it to me for £2. Came out the next week for 85p, but he still remained my favourite jock.

26. 'I'm Where It's At' Jades (Ree)
Might as well shout: 'This is Wigan Casino.' Ultimate stomper.

27. 'Ain't Nothing No Sweeter Than Love' Carl Carlton (Golden World)
Twelve-year-old Carl's song was produced by Ed Wingate and Ronnie Savoy in Detroit. Co-written by Richard (Popcorn) Wylie. Unbelievable.

28. 'Love is a Serious Business' Alfie Davidson (CBS)
Exciting inviting intro to this 70s shuffler. Just shows what depth there is in the scene.

29. 'I Just Can't Live My Life' Linda Jones (Warner Bros)
Not enough superlatives for this tremendous track. Must be one of the world's finest vocalists. Essential.

30. 'Loving on the Losing Side' Tommy Hunt (Spark)
Originally recorded on Blue Jean records by Rod Stewart sound-alikes Soul Response. Enjoyed co-producing this crossover sound and watching Tommy getting the recognition he richly deserved. I pinched the intro from 'The Love I Lost'.

31. 'Just Don't Know' Chubby Checker (Cameo)
I never tire of this Northern anthem. Real name Ernest Evans was a chicken plucker before becoming a singer. Mecca and Torch top tune. Later 'twisted' himself to fame.

32. 'Unsatisfied' Lou Johnson (Big Top)
A timeless tune distributed by New York's Bell Records. Always a floor-filler from this super-smooth soloist.

33. 'Boogaloo Party' Flamingos (Philips)
Another classic featuring the talents of Tommy Hunt. Was a club hit before charting in June 1969. Atmospheric.

34. 'Bok to Bach' Fathers Angels (Heritage)
Always loved this instrumental from Jerry Ross's own label. Rather upset when I found out they were eight white guys represented by a priest in Allentown, Pennsylvania, hence called Fathers Angels! Other 'greats' attributed to the label were Showstoppers with 'Houseparty', 'I've Been Hurt' by Bill Deal and my Wigan discoveries 'And Suddenly' by Cherry People and the Devonnes' 'Pick Up My Toy's. Great writer and producer. Lovely label.

35. 'This Old Heart of Mine' Isley Brothers (Motown)
So well known, so common, so brilliant! Always remember that it was the Torch's jock Allan Day's favourite too. Everything is just right for a perfect dancer.

36. 'I Can Take Care of Myself' Gene Chandler (Constellation)
Along with 'Mr Big Shot', I resurrected these twin turntable terrors and helped them shoot to the top of the Casino charts. Magic vinyl from the Duke.

37. 'She'll Come Running Back' Mel Britt (FIP)
Every so often a disc cuts you dead. This was one such and it still does. As popular as ever.

38. 'Turning My Heartbeat Up' MVPs (Buddah)
Have a wonderful beginning and you're three-quarters of the way there! This is utterly outstanding and just builds and builds. I chose it to open the *This England* documentary in 1977. It just absorbs you.

39. 'I Only Get This Feeling'   Chuck Jackson   (ABC)
Didn't quite make it to the top of the tree because it was too fast! Chuck's voice is definitely the business.

40. 'Here I Go Again'   Archie Bell & The Drells   (Atlantic)
Written and produced by the maestros Gamble and Huff again. Kenny Gamble gave up training as a doctor in Philadelphia in 1961 to become a singer/songwriter and he met Leon Huff when Leon was pounding the keyboard on Candy and the Kisses 'The 81' for Jerry Ross. Little did I know back in 1968, as I enjoyed Archie Bell's 'Showdown', that I'd be playing them at pool in Wigan's Bees Knees Pub in 1976, celebrating their 'Soul City Walking' hit!

41. 'Tainted Love'   Gloria Jones   (Champion)
The Northern Soul scene summed up in one record. Became the girlfriend of 70s superstar Marc Bolan, who also loved the scene. Had Marc Almond, David Ball and the handclappers in ecstasy.

42. 'You Know How to Love Me'   Phyllis Hyman   (Arista)
Mid-tempo 70s grower that crossed over to succeed in the lower end of the charts in February 1980. Divine songstress, divine song.

43. 'With This Ring'   Platters   (Musicor)
Helped the blue Pye International label become fashionable. Dedicated this sentimental stomper to my wife, Doreen, when we became engaged.

44. 'When I'm Gone'   Brenda Holloway   (Motown)
Killer 1965 Detroit sound. Almost used this to close the nighters instead of 'I'm on My Way'. Magic of Motown again.

45. 'There's a Ghost in My House' R Dean Taylor (Motown)
Possessed everything a Northern stomper could need. Brilliant opening, catchy words, places for handclapping!

46. 'End of Our Love' Nancy Wilson (Capitol)
Co-written by Nancy Wilson. Arranged and conducted by Northern legend H B Barnum. Twisted her tonsils around this mind-blowing two and a half minutes of perfection. Play it again, soon.

47. 'Seven Days Too Long' Chuck Wood (Roulette)
Another all-time favourite that I put on the other side of 'Footsee' to give it some credibility for the years to come. Mighty glad I did! Used to shake the building to its foundations.

48. 'I've Got Something Good' Sam & Kitty (JJ)
Flashbacks of where it started for me: Newtown British Legion (now JJ's Nightclub), Wigan Rugby Club and the Casino's Beachcomber. Chris Till, Lynn Halsall and Doreen doing their rude dance routine to this storming piece of vinyl.

49. 'Love You, Baby' Eddie Parker (Ashford)
Together with Williams & Watsons' 'Too Late', always reminds me of the death of the Torch and the birth of Wigan. 'Too Late' was the theme tune of the first oldies DJ I employed, Mr Personality, Martin Ellis, and 'Love You, Baby' our second oldies DJ, Dave 'Mr Torch' Evison. Both 100mph classics – so were their records!

50. 'I Walked Away' Bobby Paris (Capitol)
Describing that heartbreaking day in December 1981 when we did finally have to walk away. I relive the final night whenever I play this exceptional moody track. It almost reduces me to tears like the 'Three before Eight'. He certainly sings from the soul!

No doubt, like anyone reading this book, I can quite happily attempt to put together my favourite top fifty. The first and second ten aren't too bad, but then it seems to get harder and harder. Records possess that magical 'time tunnel' quality, which means you can instantly remember where, when and with whom you used to hear it. A piece of vinyl can unlock not only your favourite song but also that private memory.

7

If That's What You Wanted

'Ladies and gentlemen, Blackburn's Cavendish Club proudly presents the dynamic soul star, Tommy Hunt.'

Those were the words Russ Winstanley heard which opened up a new chapter in both his career and that of the man on stage. He continues the story now in his own words.

The Band struck up the Temptations' 'Get Ready' and an unbelievable soulful voice filled the enormous venue. As this lithesome figure danced on to the stage I was shellshocked. I'd never seen or heard of him before and in just thirty seconds I knew that he was a superstar. He possessed that presence that only a few artists are blessed with. His mannerisms were akin to Otis Redding's. He brought the house down with his rendition of 'My Girl'. Vocally he was similar to Chuck Jackson and Sam Cooke with the warmth of Gladys Knight rolled into one. He was even one of the best dancers I'd ever seen, back-flips, splits, etc.

I've never been as astounded or excited by an artist since. Who was this sensational singer? Where was this thirty-something soul man from? His hour and a half of music perfection brought the house down – a standing ovation for an 'unknown'. The audience wouldn't let him go.

'What a voice.'

'The best act we've ever seen.'

'I'm coming to see him again tomorrow.'

'Just wait till I tell my mates.'

Just a few of the compliments flying around after his show. I couldn't sit still. I had to meet him, but I'd be embarrassed! For the first time in my life I knocked on a dressing-room door, which was opened by an attractive blonde lady.

'I just wanted to say how much I enjoyed the show,' I stammered.

'Thank you,' she replied. 'Why don't you give Tommy twenty minutes to recover and pop back to tell him yourself?'

We returned and as we walked into his dressing room he softly said, 'Hi' and shook our hands. 'I'm Tommy and this is my wife, Sue,' he said. 'I believe you enjoyed my performance.'

'Enjoyed it! You were brilliant,' I enthused. 'No one new has ever impressed me enough to want to go backstage. Have you been singing long?'

A smile slowly lit up this coffee-coloured singer's face. 'I had a number of hits in the States in the 60s,' he replied, 'and before that a smash with the Flamingos, "I Only Have Eyes for You" and "Boogaloo Party".'

I felt that I was in a dream. 'But we play "Boogaloo Party" and lots of the Atlantic and Motown Classics that you sung tonight at our soul all-nighter, Wigan Casino.'

We both laughed and agreed that this night must have been fate.

'Otis Redding virtually brought me up. I regarded him as my uncle. I grew up with Darrell Banks, Sam Cooke, Jackie Wilson and a good friend you probably haven't heard of, Roy Hamilton.'

My jaw fell further and further open as he described being engaged to Dionne Warwick and his chart successes on Sceptre/Wand records in New York.

He recorded the never released version of 'Walk on By' and charted with the original of the Dusty Springfield hit 'I Just Don't Know What to Do with Myself', 'Human', 'I am a Witness' and 'The Door is Open'.

He'd known and worked with virtually all the legends, yet

most of the superstars hated him being on the same bill – he 'blew them away'!

It was one of those evenings that you hoped would never stop. Doreen and Sue found it highly amusing that we both couldn't talk fast enough and kept astonishing each other with singers and songs we both knew.

We were chucked out at about 4am and arranged to meet a couple of weeks later at Leigh Casino. In one chance meeting I'd found the best performer and singer I'd ever seen and someone who would also turn out to be a friend for ever.

We travelled around to see him at Wakefield Theatre and stayed over at his beautiful place in Shipley. Then I persuaded Mike Walker and Jon Smith to see him. They were knocked out as well. Tommy didn't have a recording contract then and after visiting one of our nighters he was happy to sign for Spark, with myself and Mike as his recording managers. Tommy had recognized a number of tracks at the Casino and particularly loved his close friend's 'Crackin' Up Over You' and Harold Melvin's 'Get Out'.

From the lows of trying to get out of his management contract with the disliked Johnny Francis to the highs of his return to stardom and Southport Pleasureland, it was a fascinating and rewarding relationship for everyone. We'd decided to make a cover version of 'Crackin' Up Over You'. Tommy hoped that it would give his much missed mate some more deserved recognition and his family would receive some royalties, as Roy Hamilton had penned the song himself. Golden-voiced Roy had died from cancer.

'This Tommy Hunt fella's arrived and he can't sing,' was the surprising comment from Producer Barry Kingston.

'What! Is he there? Put him on the phone.'

'Hi, Russ. Sorry about this, but I can't sing during the day! I've tried to explain to Barry that I only usually get up around 2pm and always sing at night. I'll put him back on.'

A bemused and incredulous Barry Kingston agreed to put the session back to midnight, and as I arrived at the London studio he was a happy man.

Bearded Barry blurted: 'I don't believe it. He's changed from a nonentity to one of the finest voices I've ever heard in a matter of hours. This guy is magic.'

By the time the milkman arrived we had a double-headed ready to relaunch Tommy Hunt. We ran off a number of promotional acetates for the Wigan DJs and, except for a few 'tunnel-visioned' people who said that he'd exploited the scene, the reactions were very favourable.

Dave Godin of *Blues and Soul* put the situation into perspective: 'If anyone is fully entitled to "exploit" the Northern scene then it is a black American soul singer like Tommy, since without all the thousands of black American hopefuls who nervously entered the studios to make records, there would be no Northern scene to squabble over. Anyone who's seen him perform live will already know that the man is for real. Tommy Hunt will be recognized as the major talent he is. Given time the rest of the country will soon share our secret.'

In August 1975 we sent out promotional copies and booked Tommy for our second anniversary in September. He absolutely rocked the place now everyone realized what a find he was. In October Tommy hit the charts and I went to *Top of the Pops* with him. Then, it was a case of a couple of acts had to sing live while the rest mimed. Tommy elected to sing live, which wasn't a problem except he kept mixing up the words! I stood in front of him while pointing to my 'heart' and 'tearing things apart' at the right places. He came over brilliantly. As David Essex was on the same show miming to 'Hold Me Close', Doreen was more interested in watching what he was doing!

Another coincidence was that a new release was heading for number one. 'I Only Have Eyes for You' started and Tommy sang a great version over Art Garfunkel's video.

'Hey, that's my song,' said Tommy. 'You remember, it made number one in the States when I was with the Flamingos. I'm owed around half a million pounds from the record company!'

Combined with his live act, the link with the Casino and a hit single, Tommy was heading back to the top. I was delighted. You couldn't meet a nicer fella.

Tommy Hunt's follow-up was going to be really crucial and we insisted that it should be a new song. It had to have a mid-70s feel and be acceptable to the Northern fraternity. Quite a tall order! Spark's 'in house' producer, Barry Kingston, remembered a demo by Soul Response on Blue Jean Records called 'Loving on the Losing Side'. It was done in a Rod Stewart style but he felt, given the right treatment, it could be just what we were looking for. The session was excellent and when we pinched the beginning of Harold Melvin's 'The Love I Lost' as the intro, we knew that it was a sure-fire smash.

Blues and Soul's review read: 'Ever-popular Tommy brings his recording career right up to date with this strong, strong disco item. It's particularly strong, because, for this country, it has both southern and northern appeal. The song is strong and the steady rhythm makes it ideal for the dancing folk. The chorus line reminds me of 'The Love I Lost' and that's always been a disco favourite, so that shouldn't harm its chances. Expect another crossover hit for Tommy – Top Rating (four star).'

We'd also been inundated with requests for advance copies, so we really felt that it was heading for the Top Five. There's nothing as unpredictable as the record business, though, and especially soul releases. Thousands generally fly out of specialist soul record shops and never register on the chart returns. As a lot of 'chart' shops didn't stock anything outside the Top Fifty, they could only record any 'freebies' sent them. It was a crazy and corrupt system.

We were getting rave reviews across the country and not in just northern clubs. Radio airplay was already being enjoyed via Andy Peebles on Piccadilly Radio, Chris Harper on Swansea Sound, John Green on Radio Hallam and Paul Cooke on Pennine Radio. In clubland, Paul St Field in Bournemouth reported a great reaction, together with Bob Boardman at Newcastle's Boogaloo Club and Mike Davidson at Southport's Scarisbrick Hotel.

'Loving' shot into the Top Fifty on 21 August, then moved up to the mid-thirties. Rising to number twenty-eight we had a crisis – 'Sorry, but the pressing plant's on strike!' was the astounding news from Pye. 'Shouldn't be on long though!'

Two weeks later we had to deliver the plates to CBS, but we'd already lost thousands of sales. It stayed a steady seller for months, though, and re-established our credibility within the soul fraternity. We also produced a very collectable *Live at Wigan Casino* album and then discussed the follow-up single. As well as a couple of new songs, I'd received a promotional EP from Philly records which included a very soulful but slowish track by Harold Melvin and the Bluenotes called 'Don't Leave Me This Way'. It cried out for a faster treatment in similar style to 'Loving', but no one else could see it.

Richard Searling suggested a track on a new Leo Sayer album called *How Much Love* and to reinforce his point played it a number of times at the all-nighters. We tried this but felt that it didn't work, so shelved it.

As Tommy was travelling the world and the venues were drying up in Britain, he was spending less and less time in the country. We were running out of time and a recording session had to be arranged quickly. Unfortunately I couldn't make it. Barry Kingston cut the new song, 'One Fine Morning', which was too fast even for our dancers! None of us was very keen but we needed a release so it went ahead. It limped up to number forty-four in December, but then Tommy was away touring for about eight months.

Philly finally released Harold Melvin's 'Don't Leave Me This Way', which climbed to number five in February 1977. Motown's Thelma Houston did a version which reached number thirteen a month later, in a style almost identical to how I wanted Tommy to do it! We later cut a killer ballad with Tommy for his album called *Loving You Is*, plus cover versions of 'Sign on the Dotted Line', 'You've Got Me Where You Want Me' and 'Never Can Say Goodbye'. Any of these would have made decent singles, but with Tommy away a lot and the Spark team looking to pastures new, it became difficult.

With Ian Levine virtually factory-producing singles, we looked more and more at establishing our own label. The record industry was still dominated by the ultra-rich major companies, though, and we had to break new ground to establish one of the first small, independent labels.

During 1977 Robert and Barry Kingston and Mike Walker decided to sever links with Spark and Southern Music. With the backing of music giant Boosey and Hawkes, they planned the Robert Kingston Organization, including RK Records and Publishing, based in Great Windmill Street, London. There was also an excellent studio, which was an essential part of the equation.

'If you could choose any Northern record to release at the moment, what would it be?' Mike asked.

'There isn't one, there are three. If these are made available in maxi-disc form, they'll sell for ever. They're the last three records we play before 8am. That's it, we'll call it 'Three before Eight'.

So the forerunner to Casino Classics was born. It was probably the best Northern Soul package ever produced. If you wanted a record to show the best sounds played at Wigan Casino it was here. Each had different styles, so critics who expected all thump, thump, bash were disappointed. It was difficult to choose between 'Time Will Pass You By' and 'Long After Tonight is All Over' as the A-side and radio-side. Because Jimmy Radcliffe had crept to number forty in the charts in 1965 and Dean Parrish peaked at number thirty-eight with 'I'm on My Way' in February 1975, we went with the marvellous and moody Tobi Legend. Incredible sales and, more incredibly, denied Top Twenty success because of 'regional sales' in the 'wrong shops' followed.

In April 1978 I went to the States with my wife and the winners of the Casino's holiday competition, Scotland's Alison Mitchell and Wayne McFadyen. Within a week of visiting New York, Philadelphia and Detroit, I had to discuss licensing deals for our new label. Casino Classics would be a division of RK Records, funded initially by Gerry Marshall. I would be

managing director and would move into RK's northern office in Pennington in the centre of Hindley, a couple of miles from Wigan.

While in America I did manage to see one head of a major label and asked him about licensing to stop any illegal bootlegging. I had a surprising response.

'Bootlegging saves us time and money on promotion and distribution. Tell you what. Just go away and press up some of our titles and if there's a good response we'll release them ourselves!'

'Will you put that in writing?' I inquired, trying to keep my face straight.

'What do you think?' was the reply.

No wonder there are so many people ripped off in the record business. On our return from our whirlwind trip with lots of sounds from downtown Detroit, it was time to launch Casino Classics.

Mike Walker had moved into the new premises with Casino secretary Sheila McDermott and later recruited the company accountant's wife, Vanessa McLeish, Richard Searling's wife, Judith, and Casino regular Julie Bebb. The office became the focal point of all the record business, as well as much of the day-to-day running of the Casino. It really did become a twenty-four hours a day position for me, while also jocking and selling records.

I was mainly involved in marketing, promotion and advertising, and, together with Mike, was responsible for virtually everything. The most chaotic time was when we had a new release. Around 3,000 copies were delivered from Pye and we had to mail them to radio and club DJs, magazines, newspapers, television and specialist shops.

Casino Classics' first release (CC1) was the Flirtations' version of Marvin Gaye's classic 'Little Darlin'.' Being a little bit faster, it was very much in demand. As I was licensing it from Polydor, regular Wigan jock Keith Minshull had been playing another version of Doris Troy's classic 'I'll Do Anything'. He'd 'covered it' as Lenny Gamble to hide the true identity of the singer – well-known DJ Tony Blackburn! First played as a joke, it was suddenly in demand. Polydor said there wouldn't be any problem for a release. Mentioning this to Mike and Gerry, they could see a mass of publicity backed by a nationally known radio jock, but I was very worried about credibility for both the label and the scene itself. When Tony Blackburn said that he would publicize the disc on radio and TV, that he was overjoyed he might have a hit and would let it be pressed as Lenny Gamble, I was outvoted. After almost 'blowing a fuse', they gave me the 'concession' that the Flirtations would be the A-side!

Tony appeared everywhere plugging the record and even secured a spot on *Nationwide* on BBC, hailed as the 'new king of Northern Soul'. I, like lots of other Casino lovers, cringed.

Eight thousand copies sold in the first week; surely the Flirtations were chartbound. Yep, straight in at ... number 104! Pye confirmed the news and I asked how many discs they'd sold to appear at number sixty-four. 'Just a few hundred,' was the reply, 'but these were freebies placed in the right chart shops!'

Beaten by the system again and, unfortunately, we couldn't compete with some of the record companies' marketing techniques of sending teams out to buy their own freebies, just to make sure!

Again, as with all the releases, the specialist soul shops did us proud and our releases seemed to sell for ever. The irony was that if we hadn't supplied them and just concentrated on the 500 or so 'chart-return' shops, we'd have enjoyed much more radio, television and Top Thirty success. But we decided to look after the shops who'd always supported us.

Approaching summer, I'd finally persuaded Pye to let us re-release another very big sound, 'Lost Summer Love' by Lorraine Silver. As with 'Little Darlin' ', I'd tried to choose products which had artists available to promote their songs, but I was finding it hard to trace Lorraine Silver.

Barry Collings was our main agent for the top names who appeared at the club and I was telling him about my difficulty when we were both rather astounded.

'Who is it you're trying to find?' asked Barry.

'A singer called Lorraine Silver,' I replied.

'Surely you're joking. She's my wife!'

On that happy note 'Lost Summer Love' helped renew our credibility and gave us more healthy sales, although again it didn't register in the Top Seventy-five.

Pushing for that big break and wanting a more prestigious profile, I put together probably the best release on Casino Classics: three top sounds that had been popular for quite a while. CC3 consisted of Gerri Granger's beautifully soulful mid-tempo 'I Go to Pieces', stomping Wigan favourite 'Panic' by Reparata and the Delrons and ever-popular 'Shake a Tail Feather' by James and Bobby Purify.

Much detective work found Gerri in New Jersey. She was delighted at the prospect of possibly visiting the UK and would be available for a promotional tour or television subject to the record's success.

'What are you doing at the moment, Gerri?'

'Ironing,' was the initial reply.

She'd stayed quite active as a singer and sent details of an album and recent appearances. Luckily she remembered and loved the song. We decided to 'tie-in' this release with the fifth anniversary in September 1978 and produced a souvenir sleeve including the lovely lyrics.

'I Go to Pieces' had been the fourth song before 8am and, although not an instant dancer like 'Time Will Pass You By', it was an incredible grower.

As we next hit number fifty, *Top of the Pops* promised to feature it if we again moved up the next week. Gerri was packing her bags as we waited for the call from Pye that Tuesday morning.

'It's gone down to number fifty-one', was the devastating news. We also lost *Top of the Pops*.

When we first discussed the label we dreamt of a Motown 'Hitsville' situation making and breaking new acts. Ian Levine had tried this, but the 'scene' tended to feel that he was cashing in with custom-made tracks and there was a resentment. I thought that his major mistake was producing too many at once and that his DJ spots featured too much of his own product.

As we were paying a massive percentage of royalties to the licensing labels and hadn't had that big Top Twenty yet, we weren't making any money. Les McCutcheon of Colin Bee Records fame had heard that we were looking for new artists and songs for publishing, so he came along with some promising products. To test reaction, acetates were cut of a number of songs and instrumentals. I generally chose names for the acts and instrumentals and we played 'Time Out', Autumn; 'I'm Gonna Share It with You', Diana Foster; 'Stone Soul Loving' and 'Cry Like a Child', Nicky Wilson; and two of our own, 'I Can't Seem to Hold you', Allnight Band, and 'When Love Grows Cold', Ron Grainer Orchestra.

These were released when popular and we also gained a share of the relative publishing and performing rights. After the disappointment of 'I Go to Pieces', the fourth release was by Tony Hatch's wife, Jackie Trent, and Family Affair. The titles were 'You Baby', 'Send Her Away' and 'Love Hustle', a very much requested instrumental.

We then had an explosion of Northern Soul labels fighting to reissue or cover 'wanted' tracks. Kev Roberts and Les McCutcheon were behind Nottingham-based Colony Records with a mix of 'covers' and issues of in-demand titles. Their first release was the ever-popular 'Out on the Floor' by Dobie Gray and they were distributed by Pinnacle.

In the West Midlands, Neil Rushton formed Inferno Records, fusing mainly Northern classics with soulful disco favourites such as 'Band of Gold', Freda Payne; 'Run, Baby, Run', Newbeats; 'Give Me Just a Little More Time', Chairmen of the Board; and Gil Scot-Heron's crossover 'The Bottle'.

Grapevine Records, backed by RCA, was put together by Richard Searling and his main supplier, Jon Anderson of King's Lynn's Soul Bowl. Their policy was to release only originals, but they tended to quickly 'flood' the market with 45 releases, including two compilation albums under the advertising slogan of '45 reasons to be cheerful!'

With Richard now working at RCA, they had a big advantage in being able to quickly obtain products via the RCA vaults. Although they knocked on the door of chart success with the 'poppy' monster 'What' by Judy Street (GRP 106), Grapevine was mainly aimed at the collectors – ironically the very people who moaned most about so many sounds becoming available at once. Now everybody seemed to be chasing the same sounds!

I'd tried to license the old Radio Caroline favourite 'A Touch of Velvet – a Sting of Brass' By Mood Mosaic, but EMI didn't want to know. It was a much-wanted tune again, together with 'The Theme from Joe 90'. RK's Ron Grainer was enthusiastic about being involved and had cut both instrumentals, which were readily accepted by the dancers. I also asked him to do a slightly different version of Earl Van Dyke's 'Six by Six' and another monster I'd been playing, 'The Joker'.

In December 1978, 'A Touch of Velvet' on blue vinyl reached number sixty, with fabulous sales. We also had a winner across Europe, particularly in Belgium. January 1979 saw my debut as the Wigan Joker, complete with outfit, only to peak at number fifty as the Allnight Band.

Dave Evison had joined us on radio and shop promotions and gleefully accepted his company vehicle. Until then he was famous for getting cars for around £200 and abandoning them around the country if they needed major repairs. This included a rather tasty Triumph GT6 left somewhere in Wales. Dave was an intelligent bloke who loved meeting people and sales. He'd been in charge of my stall in the Oasis, Manchester, for quite a while and, unless it was a very early start, was very reliable. He currently has his own highly successful van record sales business. You had to get used to Dave moaning, though, and finishing off everybody else's lunch!

The next releases were the ones in partnership with Les McCutcheon: double A-sides from Nicky Wilson and Diana Foster. CC9 was an absolute gem, 'How Long'. First available on a Contempo album, we licensed it immediately. Originally a hit for Ace in 1974, J J Barnes complemented the original with his wonderful vocal and crossover dance treatment. A haunting keyboard added to this recipe for success. We really thought that this would be another 'Loving on the Losing Side', but despite all efforts, it failed to get that media recognition. Dave Evison had been one of its main supporters and, together with good old Radio Luxembourg again, we'd looked forward to another winner.

J J Barnes was also well known to the scene with classics like 'Please Let Me In' and 'Our Love is in the Pocket'. He was back on Ford's production line in Detroit when I told him he might have a hit. He was overjoyed.

Ron Grainer returned with 'When Love Grows Cold' from the *Edward and Mrs Simpson* soundtrack but, as Tommy Hunt was mainly out of the country and we were still contracted to Spark, we relicensed our own track 'Loving on the Losing Side'. Together with Jason Knight's 'Our Love is Getting Stronger' and Samantha Jones's 'Stop', it was another good maxi-single.

Again we experienced good sales but not hits. The first album was a compilation of the majority of the first seven releases plus the 'Three before Eight'. It was Swansea Radio's album of the week.

Two in-demand oldies and a newie made up release number twelve, 'Surrounded by a Ray of Sunshine', 'Love Feeling' and 'I'm Your Number One'. 'Green Onions' was release number thirteen, a track from the *Quadrophenia* film and in-demand on the scene. Atlantic wouldn't let me have the original by Booker T and the MGs and label manager Jeff Grimes assured me it wouldn't be released. A session band called the Niky North Band cut us the version and we called it 'Mods '79'. After bubbling just under the Top Seventy-five in December 1979, Atlantic released the original, which reached number seven.

The second album release, *Chapter Two*, was also out at this time and contained mainly tracks not available on Casino Classics singles. It was a great success and tracks made available included 'Tainted Love' by Gloria Jones, 'It Really Hurts Me, Girl' by Carstairs, 'Better Late Than Never' by Diane Ducane, 'Sign on the Dotted Line' by Gene Latter and 'Ain't Nothing but a House Party' by the Showstoppers.

Like the other labels, 1980 saw us losing money, and when the Casino closed we finished. Tracks lined up for release were 'The Snake', Al Wilson; 'You Know How to Love Me, Phyllis Hyman; and 'This Beautiful Day', Solomon King. In a short space of time we'd become a respected label – the most successful Northern label in existence. Our ratio of hits to releases beat all the major companies.

It was fun at the time. Exasperating, disappointing, wonderful, mad and great.

Time to take a break from Russ's narrative to bring in other views of the 'coming out' of the Casino.

The Casino DJs and many Northern Soul fans were delighted at the massive exposure their music and lifestyle were getting, but inevitably there was a price to pay. Purists were annoyed a) that their exclusive music was not so secret any more, and b) the general public's chief impression of Northern Soul was a bunch of white guys (Wigan's Ovation) in tight jumpers and ridiculous pants on *Top of the Pops*.

Former Casino oldies DJ Dave Evison: 'The ironic thing was that we all wanted the whole world to hear this great music we were listening to. But when the rest of the world did, we thought it had gone too commercial. The commercialization was a good thing in the sense that it got public attention, but it gave entirely the wrong impression of the Northern scene.'

Dave actually found himself working as a rep for Casino Classics, promoting one or two singles that he would not have dreamt of playing. When Casino Classics issued 'The Theme from Joe 90', it was too much for him. His divided loyalties led to him sporting a T-shirt at the Casino saying 'Bury Joe 90' and 'Keep the Soul in Northern Soul'. Manager Mike Walker naturally took a dim view of such open rebellion and asked him to tone down his attire.

Steve Whittle was another stalwart DJ at the Casino, starting off jocking at the Beachcomber in 1974, before and after the all-nighters, and graduating to Mr M's and the main hall. It was he who played the last-ever record ('The Night') in Mr M's at the final all-nighter.

Steve stayed with the Casino to the very end, but has mixed feelings about the commercialization of the former underground scene: 'I thought it was a big mistake to let the TV cameras in. I can understand it from the Casino's point of view, and bits of the documentary are still shown on TV even today, but it brought a lot of bad stuff with it. We got a lot of wrong people coming there just because it was trendy, and there were some bad records played, like "Joe 90". Personally I didn't like all the commercialization, but I can understand why the management wanted the publicity.'

Russ bristles when faced with criticism from within the scene, both spoken and written, about the music played at Wigan. The knockers in the Casino's heyday would usually say something like: 'They play loads of records by white artists there. That's not proper Soul.' His reply is: 'It used to make me mad when I heard things like that. We would be there every week playing and discovering loads of records by black artists, but if a soulful-sounding record became popular and it turned out to be by a white artist, all we got was flak. Those kind of records were a tiny percentage of what was played at the Casino.'

Former Wigan Casino guest DJ Pep – real name Ian Pereira – says that every music scene suffers from the same problem when it goes commercial: 'Once a thing becomes commercial, every man and his dog wants to jump on the bandwagon. It's the same with any scene. I'm sure there are heavy rockers who are ashamed with some of the stuff that has crept into the charts. It won't be heavy rock in their eyes. You say to people "Northern Soul" and they say, "Oh, yeah, 'Footsee'" and all that, and then you tell them that's not what Northern Soul is all about. People get misconceptions, but that's life, really.'

And the question must be asked: would the Casino have been as famous and remembered by so many people today if there had been no 'Footsee', 'Skiing in the Snow', or TV documentary?

Would the scene still be going strong in the 1990s if there had not been an explosion of awareness of Northern Soul in the

1970s? Did the scene suffer or benefit from moving from underground to being on the lips of every teenager? It's a fascinating debate, usually conducted in good humour even today by everyone who feels passionately about the soul scene.

Part III

The People

8

Dance, Dance, Dance

Maybe it was the 'X factor' that made Wigan Casino so popular. That's either an excellent cop-out or an acknowledgement that it was the culmination of a lot of right things at the right time by the right people ... plus that elusive X factor.

There is no doubt that the DJs chosen to play to the most knowledgeable soul crowd in Britain was a crucial part of the Casino's success. Russ takes up the story again:

Probably the easiest way of running the nights would have been to employ the Blackpool Mecca DJs and Torch soul spinners on a regular basis. But I wanted it to be a new venue with new personalities and jocks stamping their own personalities on the scene. I had built up a large mail order business plus a stall on Wigan market. I already supplied a lot of the top DJs with their sounds, as well as making available the latest releases and repressings at around 85p. To alleviate my problem initially, and to stop the ever-increasing phone calls from Blackpool, I let the Mecca resident DJs Ian Levine and Colin Curtis do some guest spots after about six months.

Then a young guy with some great sounds asked for a chance to DJ. Nottingham-based Kev Roberts became Wigan's first weekly regular, earning around a tenner and usually paying £20 for a taxi for the privilege! He helped establish the foundations of a Heart of Soul for its first couple of years, before changing direction on other business commitments. Later he helped form Destiny record label and is currently managing Goldmine's releases for Tim Brown and Martyn Koppel.

Other DJs making names for themselves around the country were Frank (Ian Dewhurst), John Vincent and Steve Russell, and they were invited to join the guest roster. I then heard of a long-haired skinny guy called Richard Searling, who was making a reputation for himself at Va Va's all-nighters in Bolton. He had been building his collection through working at Global Records in Manchester and was an avid collector.

After listening to the quality sounds he had unearthed, I spoke to this shy young lad and, subject to his work commitments, he was interested in guesting at Wigan. One amusing exchange I had with Richard when he was behind the decks went like this: 'Blimey, Richard, I'm not too struck on the colour of your ale. It looks like gnat's piss.'

Richard blushed and replied: 'You're very close, really, Russ. It's difficult to get to the toilet and back in two and a half minutes, so I keep an empty pint pot in case I get caught short … and I did!'

Initially I had to get used to receiving notes of apology in Richard's highly individual writing as the all-nighters commenced, saying that due to a certain work problem he couldn't make it that night. But after a number of sessions he proved himself popular enough to become possibly my best discovery.

Prior to this, Martyn (Mr Personality) Ellis had offered his services and this highly individual and likeable lad was a massive hit as our first oldies-only jock. Manchester-based Martyn was famous for his theme tune, the Williams and Watson classic 'Too Late', and for borrowing everyone else's sounds. Together with his girlfriend Lynn Mellor, Martyn was an essential part of the Casino story.

I was now piecing together the initial parts of the jigsaw – one soul spinner committed to oldies and others who would provide a 70/30 mix of new sounds and old for us to stamp our mark on new discoveries, the Wigan sound. How could it be 'our' sounds, though, if Ian Levine and Colin Curtis of the Mecca were regulars? It would just be a further extension of the Mecca, we wouldn't have our own identity. Colin Curtis had worked only occasionally for us, but Ian Levine had visited us more frequently. He was, and still is, highly opinionated and really a non-starter for being part of a team. Too often at the Mecca he would play to an almost empty dancefloor to be first with as many new discs as possible.

The Mecca became famous for deserting the rare stomping Northern sounds and uncovering more accessible 70s and New York disco sounds. Their play-lists contained some absolute gems like the Carstairs and Anderson Brothers, but some were abysmal. I didn't want to see our scene disappear into a fashion-following disco funk direction, so I banned certain records.

Two such tunes were 'Shake and Bump' and 'Ladies Choice'. Some DJs didn't agree with me and neither did some regulars. Was I right? All I can say is that due to the change in music policy the Highland Room folded and, after reading through many people's favourite sounds, 'Shake and Bump' and 'Ladies Choice' are never featured. Nor are they ever requested. Point proved?

In 1974 Alan Rhodes from York's Hypnotique guested along with the Torch's Dave Evison and Keith Minshull, plus Manchester's Billy Paul and Warrington's Brian Rae. I had decided to feature jocks making a name for themselves across the country with the logic that it would keep us fresh to have regular new faces as well as the old faithfuls. There was method in my madness in that a successful soul spinner should have a following and it would ensure that a new batch of soulies would be inquisitive about this brilliant venue in the middle of Lancashire.

On the second anniversary, Mr M's opened as an overflow, and although I kept my eye on M's, it generally ran itself. In charge of the running order was Kenny Spence, another Wigan lad whose shape and humour were very similar to Les Dawson's. He would complain about everybody and everything before helping with any problems. Using a philosophy similar to mine – 'Don't panic' – we would take the sting out of any crisis before Gerry, and especially Mike, started flapping. Kenny was Mr Dependable with a heart of gold and it was tragic when he died so suddenly in the early 80s. Under his wing initially were Mike Rollo, Alan Cain, Bri Rigby and Steve Whittle. Every one was a born and bred Wiganer. Later Brian Rae from Warrington and Dave Evison from Stoke joined the line-up to regularly appear in both rooms. Mr M's also recruited Horwich's Stuart and Neil Brackenridge, Derek Gallagher and Billy Paul.

There was quite an amusing story about Dave Evison, who like most DJs wanted to be a Heart of Soul regular. Originally working at the Torch, he certainly had the credentials and ability to build our reputation, but I had too many jocks at the time.

'I only live in Manchester so I'll work for nothing until a vacancy arises,' argued Dave. 'I'm here every week anyway.'

I wanted to keep Dave, so I thought, 'Fair enough.' I told him: 'I'll give you a couple of quid for petrol, though, and you can share Martyn Ellis's oldies spot between 6.30am and 7.30am just before I finish off.'

Everybody was happy, or so I thought. The next thing I knew there was a headline in *Blues and Soul* over an article written by their Northern Soul correspondent, Frank Elson: 'Top DJ Dave Evison only earns a pathetic £2 for his spot at Wigan Casino.' Frank had gone for the jugular and brushed aside any attempt to check the story's validity.

Unfortunately I had to get used to this from a minority of people which both upset and disappointed me. Luckily this has been far outweighed by the hundreds of friends and acquaintances made over the years.

With Richard living just a few miles away in Bolton and working in a record shop called Tracks, he seemed the ideal choice to manage my new shop in central Wigan. Although initially rather shy, he was intelligent and knowledgeable with a good personality, and was always well presented. He was struggling to make ends meet and earned just £10 a week. His wife, Judith, worked as a waitress at Smithills Coachhouse to help pay the mortgage on their terraced house. The soul spinner abandoned his further education plans to marry Judith and provide for their daughter, Carolyn.

I doubled his wage to give him a decent living and got him a few extra quid working with me on the Friday early sessions. After his initial apprehension, a full-time occupation in the record business proved to be the best move of his life. It led to his job as a plugger with RCA records in 1978 and, of course, a successful career as a radio and clubland DJ. After being a buyer with Makro, the wholesalers, for many years, he now works in a similar capacity with a Warrington-based wholesaler.

Obviously we had our arguments, but both of us believed passionately in what we were doing and neither of us could be blamed for sometimes being stubborn or dogmatic. In fact, I felt that the regular 'heated debates' helped us to appreciate other points of view. Although we may have trodden different paths we had the same goal: to make and keep the Casino at number one and dedicate our lives to the music and the scene. We never ever uttered that maxim, but it was definitely true.

Our different approaches and attitudes helped us to gel, and even though we loved many of the same sounds we each had other favourites, which meant that as a combined package we were unbeatable! It is regrettable that Richard did not feel he could cooperate with this book, but he must have his reasons.

In 1977, Billy Paul, Martyn Ellis and John Vincent finished. Alan Rhodes left in early 1979 and his spot was initially shared between Soul Sam and Pat Brady. Other soul spinners to grace the stage were Midlander Chris King, later to front the KWS band, Shaun Gibbons, who founded the Morecambe Pier all-nighters, Rod Looker and Gary Rushbrooke.

In 1974 the Casino started to become the centre of the soul universe and I was by then receiving far too many sounds to play and break. We had to have a plan to establish the Wigan sound and weekly meetings became imperative. A play-list was discussed and as I possessed the majority of the best vinyl, the

SOUTHERN Enquiries: Phone
PORTSMOUTH 832765

O

Owing to the success of the first two coach trips to

WIGAN CASINO

It is to become a once monthly trip, starting on the 11th of
January. The coach will leave Portsmouth at 5.30 p.m., picking
up at Winchester, Newbury and Oxford. The fare for the trip is
£3. Anyone interested please get in contact as soon as possible.

U

c **L** UB **40 HASLEMERE ROAD, SOUTHSEA,
PORTSMOUTH**

other DJs were only too happy to borrow and play them. They
would get first shout at any spare copies or acetates of the top
sounds. This way we would all pull in a similar direction. The
four 'main' jocks would spin four chosen tunes twice during
each spot and an additional four discs were added each week.
We discussed the progress or popularity of these songs every
week and whether to drop any if there was a poor response, or
when to reduce it to one play per session.

This way we had people leaving the club with a number of
new sounds going around in their heads. Most of the sounds
were exclusive to the Casino and could not be heard anywhere
else in the country. This exclusivity was a major reason for the
success of the Casino and the scene in general. You *had* to go
there to find out what was happening. You could perhaps read
about these titles in *Blues and Soul*, but unless you went you
would not know what they were like. As each new spin became
more and more popular, I would probably receive a few more
copies, which were sold to other DJs. The fact that these records
were never hits in the States, usually in the mid- to late-60s, kept
them rare and £50 to £100 (at 1970s prices, don't forget!) was
quite common for a top tune.

Some jocks or collectors would sometimes make illegal
acetates, usually called Emi discs, of these rare records, with the
first-generation duplicates bringing around £10 to £20,
dropping to £5 with an in-demand record on the other side.

Everyone's American connections would by now be hunting for this new 'monster' in the States, and with illegal copies being produced a record might well start to be heard in many of the smaller Northern Soul clubs throughout the UK. Within a minimum of three months, a brand-new 'first spin' at the Heart of Soul could be being requested in a Bournemouth or Aberdeen record shop.

As soon as the artist or label was clarified, specialist wholesalers like John Bratten's Select-a-Disc in Nottingham would approach the record company in the States for an initial 'special pressing' of 3,000, which would arrive in England to retail for about £1. Most of the British record companies were unaware of this team of knowledgeable black-music lovers rediscovering discarded gems that the companies had been unable to break. It was unheard of, DJs using their talents to put forgotten artists back into the charts instead of the acts or the company being the driving force.

We weren't the first to do this. Manchester's Twisted Wheel had brought many Motown, Atlantic, Stax and Chess gems to the attention of the music press and pirate stations. Without unique DJs like the Wheel's Roger Eagle, these labels would never have had much chart success, as BBC radio branded them as disco records! Now they form the basis of the majority of people's record collections and most of the play-lists of 'Gold' radio stations.

Stoke's all-nighters, the Torch and Blackpool Mecca's Highland Room also flew the flag for our favourite music and aided the success of tremendous artists like Edwin Starr, Martha Reeves, Major Lance, Jackie Wilson and Frankie Valli.

Contrary to what many people thought at the time, the Casino did not have a bottomless pit of money to bring across live acts from the States. Most popular acts would charge around £2,500 a show, and £3,000 was the limit set by the Casino management. Therefore the Station Road venue was never able to bring its army of followers acts like the Four Tops and Marvin Gaye.

Popular artists attracted many people to the Casino, but also

WIGAN CASINO
ALL-NIGHTER

★ ★ ★ ★ ★ ★

VISIT THE HEART OF SOUL
EVERY SAT. / SUNDAY MORNING 2 a.m. — 8 a.m.

Featuring the No 1. Soulspinners
RUSS, KEV and RICHARD
PLUS Martin Ellis and lots of top guest DJs playing such great sounds as:

Sidrus theme (Explosion) instr; Condition Red; Build Your House—Gwen & Ray; Let It Be You Babe (instr)—Music Box; Lovebound (instr)—Audio Art Strings; Porky & the Monarchs; 6 x 6 (new version); Johnny Vonelli; Sister Lee—Sam Ward; I Can't Get Enough (instr); Ain't No Soul (instr); Strings A Go Go—Bob Wilson; They Say (instr); Breakaway—Steve Karman Band; Stop, Look Listen—Tikis; Can't Help Lovin' You—Johnny Caswell; What About The Music (instr); Sam & Kitty (instr); Connie Stevens; Land; McNeil; Dynamics; John Fucien.

As our regular members know we play the biggest and rarest sounds first—that's why we are so popular

---

SATURDAY JULY 20
ON STAGE AT APPROX. 9 p.m. ——— THE INCREDIBLE
R. DEAN TAYLOR
THE "GHOST IN MY HOUSE" MAN
7.30 — 1.30 (Membership not required for early session) Admission £1 before 10 p.m., 60p after

---

Members only—lots of food— soft drinks—breakfasts
great dance floor

★★★★★★★★★★★★★★★★★★★★★★★★★★★★★★★★★★★★

DON'T MISS OUT ON OUR
TWO GREAT BADGES

THIS IS THE AUTHENTIC WIGAN CASINO BADGE, FROM THE CLUB ITSELF. BEWARE OF IMITATIONS ADVERTISED ELSEWHERE.

60p each— plus s.a.e.

Both fully embroidered—actual size 3½in diameter

★★★★★★★★★★★★★★★★★★★★★★★★★★★★★★★★★★★★

TO JOIN OUR CLUB,
SEND FORM BELOW TO ARRIVE AT LEAST 48 HOURS BEFORE YOU DO

Post to: **WIGAN CASINO SOUL CLUB, STATION ROAD, WIGAN WN1 1YQ, LANCASHIRE**
W.C.S.C. APPLICATION FORM FOR MEMBERSHIP

! (name) ....

of (address) ....

do apply for membership to Wigan Casino Soul Club. I am over 18 years of age and agree to abide by the rules of the club.

P.S. Don't forget Beachcomber Soul Snack Bar open from 12 midnight—2a.m. and from 8a.m.—10a.m. for breakfasts (adj. Casino entrance) deterred others from going. For one thing the admission price had to be raised to recoup the cost of paying the performer, and sometimes the act booked might have appeared elsewhere in the country as part of a tour.

Russ confirmed such mixed feelings about the occasional live shows which punctuated the Saturday all-nighters: 'Each time we had an act on, as many people stayed away as were attracted to the all-nighter. The admission price was higher, some people weren't into live acts, and we had to be careful not to pick anyone who was touring the country. What was the point of someone travelling to Wigan if, say, they could see Junior Walker closer to home a few weeks later? Personally, although I loved the live acts, the shows and the dancing competition sometimes interrupted the flow of the all-nighters.

★

One artist who certainly caused a stir when he graced the hallowed stage of the Casino was a certain R Dean Taylor. Back in the charts owing to the success of 'Ghost in My House', the Motown artist toured Britain in 1974.

'Ghost in My House', as mentioned already, was a 1967 track used as a filler on a 99p *Music for Pleasure* album released in 1973. The album was put out to capitalize on his 1968 number seventeen hit 'Gotta See Jane' and 'Indiana Wants Me', number two in 1971.

Originally a writer for Motown with hits for the Four Tops like 'I'll Turn to Stone' and the Supremes' 'Love Child', he co-wrote 'Ghost' with the legendary Holland/Dozier/Holland team.

Regular plays of 'Ghost in My House' at the Casino led to Motown being astonished at the sale of the 99p album. Another slice of luck for them was that R Dean Taylor's 'Let's Go Somewhere' had turned up on their VIP subsidiary label in 1965. Motown finally got their act together and released 'Ghost' with 'Let's Go Somewhere' on the B-side in April 1974. It stayed in the charts for fifteen weeks, peaking at number two, and R Dean Taylor was booked to appear at an early Saturday night session at the Casino.

Ironically he wouldn't appear at the all-nighter, but the Casino was not too perturbed, as he had only had the two Northern Soul-style hits.

R Dean Taylor's arrival at the Casino brought Russ a legendary phone call at home from a flustered Gerry Marshall: 'Russ, R Dean Taylor's arrived. There must be a mistake. He's not black!'

Russ had forgotten to tell Gerry that the performer was the first white man to have a hit with Tamla Motown. Understandably, many people had their illusion shattered when they saw him in the flesh!

★

The trouble with a music scene that revolves around rare and long-forgotten recordings is that sometimes the artists themselves have difficulty remembering their lesser-known songs! Just because an obscure single is popular with eccentric Brits at dubious all-night clubs in England does not guarantee that the artist who cut it in Detroit thirty years previously will remember and love it to the same degree.

This is what happened when Motown recording star Martha Reeves was booked to appear live at the Casino. Martha and the Vandellas had, of course, massive hits with 'Dancing in the Streets', 'Jimmy Mack', 'Nowhere to Run', etc. But the contrary Casino-goers liked rarer outings than that, and in their usual fashion latched on to her Motown recording 'One Way Out'.

The single had made little impact on the charts in the mid-1960s and more than a decade later Martha could barely remember it. What was worse, her backing band did not know the song at all. But Martha is a true professional and got round the problem magnificently during her live show.

Russ recalled: 'She had heard of the Casino and was happy to play there. Like all the acts, she had a look through the stage curtain and saw this mass of people and was knocked out. She was even video-taping the show for the people back home.'

Russ warned Martha that the fans would expect her to sing 'One Way Out' in addition to her hits and sure enough, after a few numbers, the shouts from the crowd began: 'Sing "One Way Out"!'

Martha realized that she wasn't going to get away without singing it. So in a break during the show she listened to the song on headphones and said: 'Yes, I remember this now.' Then she went on stage and sang the whole song, word perfect, without any backing. The crowd loved it, even if her backing band looked a little bemused!

★

Sax supremo Junior Walker, who sadly died in November 1995 at the age of fifty-three, after a long battle with cancer, was also a firm favourite of the Casino crowd. The Motown creator of worldwide hits like 'Road Runner', 'Shotgun', 'How Sweet It Is', etc. appeared live at the Casino on several occasions. The sax-playing soul star was never less than a wow with the crowd and could hold a 2,000-plus audience in the palm of his hand.

Russ said: 'He always brought the house down but away from the stage he was very shy and retiring. He didn't say much to anyone, he just did his job and then went. And he was note perfect.'

★

Few soul performers have survived the decades since the 1960s better than Edwin Starr. He is still very much in demand at venues large and small around the country, and never turns in less than a quality performance. With a string of hits behind him

WIGAN CASINO ALL~NIGHTER

VISIT THE HEART OF SOUL
Every Sat. Night/Sun Morning Midnight-8am

FEATURING THE COUNTRY'S NO. 1 SOUL SPINNERS

RUSS WINSTANLEY & RICHARD SEARLING

Plus Top regular Guest D.J.s KEITH MINSHULL, PEP, BRIAN RAE, ALAN RHODES, DAVE EVISON etc and other top guest soul spinners. (Featuring two floors with KENNY SPENCE, BRIAN, STUART & GAL in Mr. M's playing THE OLDIES) • NORTHERN SOUL nights every Wednesday (7.30-11 p.m.) and Friday (7.30-11 p.m.) •Featuring RUSS & STUART (NO MEMBERSHIP REQUIRED). Also early Saturday in Mr. M's (7.30 p.m.-11 p.m.) with 3 Top Guest Soul Spinners

SAT/SUN, MARCH 24th
Midnight — 8 a.m.

From America —

The Incredible

MARVELETTES

(on stage approx. 3.30 am)

Admission £2.75
Members ONLY
PAY AT DOOR

SAT/SUN APRIL 14th
MIDNIGHT — 8 a.m.

THE ELGINS

(on stage approx. 3.30 a.m.)

Admission £2.50
Members ONLY
PAY AT DOOR

Don't forget first Friday of every month is
THE OLDIES ALL-NIGHTER
Come and listen to those memories
Friday night/Sat. Morning, Midnight-8am

NEXT OLDIES ALL-NIGHTER APRIL 6th. Admission £1.75 (Members ONLY)

TO BECOME A MEMBER   YOU MUST BE OVER 18 — MEMBERSHIP IS NOW 25p
Applications to arrive 48 hrs. before you do. Please send SAE

WIGAN CASINO SOUL CLUB.
STATION ROAD, WIGAN
WN1 1YQ, LANCASHIRE
W.C.S.C. APPLICATION-
FORM FOR MEMBERSHIP...

I (name) _____

of (address) _____

DO APPLY FOR MEMBERSHIP TO WIGAN CASINO SOUL CLUB. I AM OVER 18 YEARS OF AGE AND AGREE TO ABIDE BY THE RULES OF THE CLUB like 'SOS' ('Stop Her on Sight'), 'Headline News', '25 Miles', 'War', etc., the former Ric Tic and Motown star has a brilliant repertoire.

He also appeared several times at the Casino and still pops up at Northern Soul all-nighters even today. Equally at home wandering around a club chatting to the knowledgeable record collectors and on stage, Edwin is a prolific performer who appeals to all age groups.

Said Russ: 'There are very few performers like Edwin who can do it for anybody. If he played to a group of pensioners he would still go down a storm. When they had the Giants of Motown show, they would put Edwin on before the "major" acts and he would bring the house down. Some of the better-known acts who had to follow him weren't as good live. He was unique in that he also played the Wheel and the Torch before the Casino and he was one of the first acts we ever had.'

For the Casino management and crowd it was pleasing to see Edwin back in the charts in 1979 with 'Contact'. It soared to number six in the charts after weeks of being heavily played by all the soul clubs and eventually the pop discos. It gave a well-earned revival to his recording career, and the follow-up single, 'Happy Radio', also made it to number nine. For Russ: 'It was nice to return the compliment to Edwin after all the pleasure he had given us. He had been a bit in the wilderness for a few years and it was good to see him have some current success.'

Soul lovers will also recognize the backing band he brought with him from the States for a Casino performance. 'You won't have heard of them, but they're called Rose Royce and they are going to be huge,' he told Russ one night. He was right: in the late 1970s that same group had major chart success with 'Car Wash', 'Wishing on a Star', and 'Love Don't Live Here Any More'.

★

Not every act at the Casino was rapturously received. An eagerly awaited appearance was by former Okeh recording artist Billy Butler, whose 'Right Track' was, and still is, a Northern Soul anthem. He stormed on stage to a great reception, played 'Right Track', and then took the crowd through some of his lesser-known material. None of it was in the stomping 60s vein that appealed to Casino-goers and interest soon began to wane. People started to sit down on the floor and chat to each other. Finally Billy, sensing that he was dying out there, said: 'I think I'm going to go now before we all get really bored,' and walked off to sympathetic applause.

★

Lots of acts split up, re-form and add new members to their line-ups and someone retains the legal right to use the name of the band. One of those chameleon-like bands was Motown stars the Marvelettes. They had early success for Berry Gordy with 'Please, Mr Postman' and later cut several Northern Soul-loved sides, including 'Only Your Love Can Save Me' and 'Destination Anywhere' (featured in the film *The Commitments*).

The original line-up was Gladys Horton, Wanda Young, Georgeanna Tillman, Katherine Anderson and Juanita Cowart, but bear in mind that it was probably fifteen years later that they appeared at the Casino. Could *you* recognize and name the ladies involved? The Marvelettes played live twice at the Casino, going down well on both occasions.

On the second occasion, Russ chatted to the girls before, stage curtains opened. He said: 'It's packed again. Looks like it's going to be brilliant, just like last time.'

The girls replied: 'Oh, that wasn't us last time.'

★

Packed all-nighters at the Casino.

Going home after an all-nighter: outside the club and (*below*) exchanging records on Wigan station. (*Dave Motler*)

Filming for Tony Palmer's *This England* documentary in 1977 (*above*) (*Granada*) and former dance champion Sandy Holt, who is now a martial arts expert (*below*).

Out on the floor at the Casino's famous all-nighters. (*Wigan Observer*)

The fans cheer Tommy Hunt in 1975 (*above*) and enjoy an anniversary reception (*below*). Anna Ford (*front left*) was an early fan.

Just a few of the Casino regulars (*clockwise, from top left*): Hank and Tommy Cockburn of Falkirk, Andrew and Fiona Nevin (*Wigan Observer*), some of the St Anne's crowd and a group of entrants for one of the Casino's dance competitions.

The last days of the Casino: Russ Winstanley after the fire (*below*) and (*above*) only the piano remains as the bulldozers move in. (*Wigan Observer*)

The authors, David Nowell (*left*) and Russ Winstanley (*right*), on the Casino site today (*above*) and (*below*) the all-nighter lives on at the Ritz in Manchester. (*Manifesto*)

It's difficult to mention Major Lance without immediately thinking of the Torch. The album *Major Lance Live at the Torch*, which captured all of the excitement of the famous Okeh recording artist's show and the Stoke-on-Trent venue, was a landmark in the promotion of the underground Northern Soul scene.

But Major Lance also appeared at the Casino, and how many artists could chose from his vast range of soul favourites, like 'Ain't No Soul', 'Investigate', 'You Don't Want Me No More', etc., etc.? It was a little like Junior Walker and Edwin Starr in that people always said they had already seen their shows, but were never disappointed a second, third or fourth time. One of the highlights of Major Lance's show at the Casino was when his friend Tommy Hunt joined him on stage for a song.

★

Of all the artists who appeared at the Casino, the one Russ awaited more eagerly than any other was the great Jackie Wilson. 'I Get the Sweetest Feeling', 'Higher and Higher', 'Nothing but Blue Skies', 'Reet Petite' – the list of his successful Brunswick recordings goes on and on. Russ was trying to interview Jackie for *Black Echoes* before the show and discovered that he wasn't feeling too well.

Jackie went on stage in his leather suit and showed what a great star he was and left the crowd calling for more. But amidst the adulation, many people felt that his voice did not sound as strong as they had expected. 'This is the only place I've known to rival the atmosphere of the Apollo in New York. Everyone's so knowledgeable of black music. I can't wait to return.' Jackie had said.

Soon afterwards, on his return to the States, Jackie fell into a coma, in which he remained for several years before finally dying in 1984. His illness and death were mourned by his colleagues in the music business the world over, not least by Casino-goers, who had witnessed one of his final shows.

WIGAN CASINO
ALL-NIGHTER
VISIT THE HEART OF SOUL
EVERY SAT. NIGHT / SUN. MORNING 1.30 a.m.—8 a.m.
FEATURING THE COUNTRY'S NO. 1
SOUL SPINNERS

RUSS WINSTANLEY & RICHARD SEARLING
PLUS TOP REGULAR GUEST D.J.s JOHN VINCENT, KEITH MINSHULL, FRANK, PEP, SOUL SAM, DAVE EVISON ETC. (FEATURING TWO FLOORS WITH MIKE ROLO, ALAN, KENNY & GUESTS IN MR. M's PLAYING THE OLDIES)
NORTHERN SOUL NIGHTS EVERY WEDNESDAY (7.30—11 p.m.) and FRI-DAY (7.30—12 Midnight)
FEATURING RUSS & RICHARD (NO MEMBERSHIP REQUIRED)

SAT. NIGHT / SUNDAY MORNING 1.30 a.m. — 10.00 a.m.

APRIL 26
FROM AMERICA THE SENSATIONAL

BETTY WRIGHT
+ 10 PIECE ALL AMERICAN BAND ON STAGE APPROX. 3.30 a.m.

MEMBERS ONLY

MAY 10th ALL NIGHTER
THE SENSATIONAL

JACKIE WILSON

KEEP THE FAITH *'HEART OF SOUL' *'NIGHT OWL' **Badges available 60p each plus SAE**
Car Stickers available, 30p each plus S.A.E. Also original 'Allnighter' Posters approx 20in. x 30in. in 4 colours 50p each plus large S.A.E.

TO JOIN OUR CLUB (FREE MEMBERSHIP) SEND FORM BELOW TO ARRIVE AT LEAST 48 HOURS BEFORE YOU DO.

Post to: WIGAN CASINO SOUL CLUB, STATION ROAD, WIGAN WN1 1YQ, LANCASHIRE
W.C.S.C. APPLICATION FORM FOR MEMBERSHIP

! (name) ....

of (address) ....

do apply for membership to Wigan Casino Soul Club. I am over 18 years of age and agree to abide by the rules of the club.

(P.S. Don't forget Beachcomber Soul Snack Bar open from 12 midnight to 2 a.m. and 8 a.m. — 10 a.m. for breakfasts (adj. Casino entrance)

Russ said: 'I loved his voice, and songs like 'I Get the Sweetest Feeling' were always among my favourites. He was good at Wigan, but not quite as good as I had expected. He wasn't feeling well then and it was tragic when he went home and fell into a coma. Jackie Wilson had one of the great voices of all time.'

★

The Detroit Emeralds appeared not at an all-nighter at the Casino but, unusually, at a Sunday all-dayer. The smooth soulsters were famous for their hits 'Feel the Need in Me' and 'You Want It You Got It', but stunned the audience with an entire show of songs with a 60s stomping feel. They knew exactly what the Casino crowd wanted – and made sure they got it!

★

'Here I Go Again' by Archie Bell and the Drells was a super commercial song loved by all-nighter-goers and pop fans. So it was a disappointment that on the one occasion they appeared at the Casino, they didn't sing it.

The group were back in the charts with 'Soul City Walking' and did a fine spot of 70s and 60s material at the Casino, before preparing to travel down the road to the Ritz all-dayer in Manchester for another show twelve hours later.

Russ remembered: 'They were very good, but I was a little disappointed they didn't do "Here I Go Again". They were staying in Wigan at the Grand and on the Sunday we went to the Bees Knees pub and me and Steve Connor challenged them to a game of pool. The barman asked us who the black guys we were playing against were and I said: "Archie Bell and the Drells." He said: "Oh, yeah," like he didn't believe me!'

★

While compiling this book, the authors have come to a surprising conclusion: of all the live acts who appeared at the Casino, Betty Wright appears by popular consensus to have put on the best show.

Hardly a household name in the Northern Soul fraternity until her Wigan show, Betty took the audience by the scruff of the neck, shook them up and threw them into raptures no one had expected. Her stage presence, her voice, her energy, the perfect sound mixing of her large backing band and the reaction from the crowd have ensured her show will never be forgotten.

The diminutive singer with the Afro hair-do was having some chart success with 'Where is the Love?', which had been played at the Casino, and the Casino DJs were also playing 'Love don't Grow on a Love Tree' from the same album. Russ found her shortly before the show sucking an orange and complaining croakily of a sore throat and a cold. But any misgivings he might have had about the show were dispelled the moment she burst on to the stage.

'When she came across here she hadn't really been heard of, so we didn't have very high expectations. But she was absolutely fabulous and her band was excellent,' said Russ.

Betty found a legion of new fans that night and, judging by the reaction from DJs and punters alike, gave probably the best live show the all-nighters ever saw.

★

Gloria Jones of 'Tainted Love' and 'Heartbeat' fame was another fine act who graced the Casino's stage. Her boyfriend was, of course, Marc Bolan. Marc did not accompany her to the Casino, but Russ later met him when he was appearing on a TV show. They chatted about music and it emerged that Marc was a big soul fan and had a great knowledge of Stax and Atlantic and 60s soul. Gloria was at the wheel of the car when it tragically overturned in 1979, trapping and killing the T Rex superstar.

★

So what of the acts the Casino never saw? The Wigan venue had always wanted to put on the Tavares. The group had had giant crossover hits with 'Heaven Must be Missing an Angel', 'Don't Take Away the Music' and 'It Only Takes a Minute', and the Casino had them lined up to play the fourth anniversary. But when they found out it was an all-nighter they wouldn't do it.

It was also Russ's ambition to put on the O'Jays, but they usually came as part of the Philly show with Billy Paul and the Intruders and would have been beyond the Casino's budget.

Then there was the sorry tale of James Brown. Yes, the Godfather of Soul was once booked to appear at the Casino, but the ambitious move was doomed to failure. He was doing a European tour and found he had two empty diary dates. His agent phoned up the Casino and offered his services for one night. Because the funky Godfather was not considered appropriate for the all-nighter, the Casino gladly booked him for a special Sunday night show. So, at two weeks' notice, the Casino started advertising the gig to a sceptical world. Once people were sure it was not a hoax, word spread quickly and final arrangements were made for a famous occasion.

The James Brown crew drove back from the Continent through the night and arrived in Wigan in the afternoon to set up their equipment. That evening 1,500 fans crowded into the Casino to see the show – not a sell-out, but a fine attendance considering the short notice.

Russ's pulse started to race when a luxury coach with blackened windows pulled up. One of James Brown's giant minders appeared and beckoned to Russ to approach. The nervous DJ was summoned into the great man's presence and asked: 'Is the club full?'

'There are 1,500 people in but the club holds a lot of people,' Russ replied.

'I'll go and have a look,' replied the performer.

So James Brown and his entourage went into the club and peered over the balcony.

The Godfather assessed the situation and said: 'Nope, there's not enough people in.' And with that he went straight back to the coach and it drove away, leaving the Casino management, 1,500 fans and a bunch of tired roadies very upset.

All the fans were given a refund and the roadies kicked hell out of the equipment in their anger and frustration.

★

Simply Red singer Mick Hucknall, possessor of one of the most soulful voices in pop music, enjoyed going to dance events in the Greater Manchester area in the early 1980s. He is reputed to have visited the Casino's 'early' sessions, as opposed to the all-nighter.

He told the BBC programme *The Whistle Test* during a feature on Northern Soul and the all-nighters of the 1980s: 'I think there was a lot of camaraderie there and a lot of people knew each other through those clubs and got to get hold of the records. I've never even been to a Wigan all-nighter, but I've been to an all-nighter and it seems that everybody knew everybody … pretty much the same as the early punk gigs. Most of the people in Manchester knew each other around that period. It was almost like a bizarre little family … and it was really orientated towards dancing.'

★

M People, Kylie Minogue and Wigan Casino might seem strange bedfellows. But Northern Soul is the common thread, largely due to a Blackpool musician called Mark Bell.

Mark was one of the founders of M People before leaving to become in-house producer for Deconstruction Records, the top-selling dance label and subsidiary of RCA. The Blackpool music scene, and Northern Soul in particular, was one of his greatest influences: 'Blackpool was one of the birthplaces of Northern Soul and it was also a top area for jazz funk. I was influenced by three guys from here who just personified club culture – Ian Levine (of Blackpool Mecca), who used to bring in records from America, Chris Lowe of the Pet Shop Boys and Soft Cell's David Ball.'

Mark duetted with Heather Small of M People on the group's single 'Don't Look Any Further', from the album *Elegant Slumming*. He also worked on three songs for their earlier collection, *Northern Soul*.

He then found himself writing a song for Kylie Minogue's 1994 album, *Don't Hold Back*. He was in illustrious company, as Prince and Lenny Kravitz both contributed to the album too. One of the surprise tracks that Kylie recorded under his guidance was a certain 'Time Will Pass You By'. Yep, the very same song that was one of the famous 'Three Before Eight'!

★

In the Casino's latter days, one of the more 'modern' sounds played there was 'The Only Way is Up' by Otis Clay. It later became a monster at venues like Clifton Hall in Rotherham. Imagine Northern Soul fans' surprise many years later to find it re-recorded and given the full disco treatment by Yazz. It shot to number one and shot her to fame.

★

One of the people who used to ask Russ at the Casino to play 'Tainted Love' by Gloria Jones was a young skinny guy called Marc Almond. The pacey, mid-60s Ed Cobb song was one of the most popular Northern Soul discoveries of the 1970s and for many fans was the epitomy of the genre. One night in 1980 Marc told Russ that he and his friend David Ball had formed a group and recorded a version of 'Tainted Love'. That group was Soft Cell, and their electronic dance version of 'Tainted Love' gave them a worldwide number one hit. Soft Cell also went on to record another Casino biggie, Judy Street's 'What?'.

Marc and David had met at Leeds Art College and, according to their own press releases: ' ... shared a love of Northern Soul and Tamla Motown. In late 1979, they started performing together in seedy clubs. The show was like Tommy Cooper backing Larry Grayson doing a bad impersonation of Shirley Bassey.' Enough said!

★

To a generation of all-nighter-goers, Dexys were naughty substances (Dexedrine) which some dancers took to help them through the night. To pop fans of the early 1980s Dexys were a group fronted by Kevin Rowland.

Dexys Midnight Runners (just think about the name for a second) were a heavily soul-influenced band who made a single as a tribute to the much-loved club performers Geno Washington and the Ram Jam Band. The catchy chorus of 'Geno' helped catapult the single to number one in the British charts and brought them a new and wider audience.

The album *Searching for the Young Soul Rebels* also included a version of the Northern Soul anthem 'Seven Days Too Long', the Chuck Wood song which ironically Russ had placed as the B-side to the infamous 'Footsee' single in 1974.

Dexys had wanted to perform Geno live at the Casino, but the venue's management turned them down. However, Kevin Rowland did visit the all-nighters.

★

'And here is the news, with Anna Ford.'

As you see her face on TV it is not normally one you would associate with Wigan Casino, but Anna did indeed visit those sweaty, packed all-nighters on more than one occasion. She was a young, ambitious TV reporter with Granada when the Casino

MR GEORGE'S NIGHT CLUB
COVENTRY
Every Sunday Night 7-30 till 11-30
ALL DRINKS HALF PRICE
PETE WATERMAN D.J.
Playing sounds like Bobby Paris, Bob Relf, Jimmy (Soul) Clark, Sam and Kitty, Vibrations, April Stevens, Rose Battles, Hogy Lands, and now for something completely different fry Bok to Bach, Black is Black, Music To My Ears, Hit And Run, Shing-A-Ling, Oh Linda, Save The Last Dance (not D. Joe)? Up tight Eddie's my name. It's no really. Anyway there's more if ya wants it. So join our brothers and sisters from Burton, Stoke, Birmingham, Leeds, Nuneaton, Hinchley and wait for it Brighton. Nice one! Become a Coventry Kid.

was at its peak and used to visit the venue with colleagues, including music fan Tony Wilson.

Each anniversary the Casino used to invite VIPs to a buffet and a few drinks before the ceremonial cutting of the cake on stage, and Anna and others were among the chosen few.

'She loved the place,' said Russ. 'Tony Wilson was interested in all types of music and she used to tag along with him.' And just to prove it, elsewhere in this book you will find a picture of Anna taken at one of the anniversary celebrations.

★

The record-producing team of Stock, Aitken and Waterman is referred to as the 'hit factory' of the 1980s, echoing the massive success of the Tamla Motown songwriters and producers of two decades earlier.

Commercial soul influences can be heard in many of their hit records for artists like Kylie Minogue, Rick Astley and Jason Donovan. That's hardly surprising, as Pete Waterman was a Northern Soul DJ.

Pete was resident DJ at Coventry Tiffany's in the 1970s and found himself alongside Casino DJ Kev Roberts. Among the other venues the then less-than-famous Mr Waterman worked was Mr George's Night Club, also in Coventry. A glance at his play-list demonstrates that he had a deep knowledge of the Northern Soul scene. Pete popped up elsewhere in the early 1970s, writing for *Blues and Soul* about the Philadelphia sound, he was pictured with legendary producer Leon Huff.

Pete was also a record dealer and is understood to have

attended the Casino all-nighters even before the Wigan venue reached its height of fame.

Gradually his love of music took him into record producing. The pop/soul influence is very apparent on many of the Stock, Aitken and Waterman productions, and it was Pete himself who once said in a magazine interview: 'I'm positive that *Saturday Night Fever* was based on Wigan Casino.'

That remark was repeated to the Casino crowd to great cheers, but the claim is impossible to prove. In the smash-hit film, John Travolta played a young working-class lad in a dead-end job who became a 'somebody' at weekends when he danced at his local disco. It could be a sanitized, Americanized, pop version of a thousand guys who went to Wigan Casino. Draw your own conclusions!

★

Another star rumoured to have attended the all-nighters is Paul Weller. The former Jam frontman, now a successful solo artist, brought his band to the midweek Casino punk nights and is reputed to have returned to see what the all-nighters were all about.

Soul influences can be heard in his recordings, particularly on the Motownesque 'A Town Called Malice', which has been compared to The Supremes' 'You Can't Hurry Love'.

★

What's the connection between a worldwide number one and a Northern Soul DJ? A gentleman by the name of Chris King, that's who.

Chris, an occasional guest at the Casino and a regular DJ and promoter in the Midlands, was the brains behind the group KWS, who in 1992 had a smash hit with 'Please Don't Go'. The lifelong soul fan turned record producer had put his hand to churning out rave records in a Birmingham studio with another well-known Northern Soul promoter Neil Rushton.

Then in just four hours they turned in 'Please Don't Go', an up-tempo version of the old KC and the Sunshine Band hit. Within two months it was number one in the UK charts and went on to chart success in thirty different countries.

Now Chris is back on the Northern Soul scene again, promoting venues, DJing at places like the Ritz and enjoying getting back to his roots. He explained that the momentum caused by the success of KWS had taken three and a half years to subside: 'We were doing tours with Alexander O'Neil and shows in Mexico City in front of 50,000 people. We picked up a double platinum album in Australia, double gold in America, gold in Britain, you name it.'

So why is he back on the scene again?

Chris replied simply: 'The Northern scene has always been a hobby, regardless of anybody's views on monies made. I guarantee that every penny I've ever made out of Northern Soul I've either spent on records or lost on bad promotions. You've got to do it because you bloody well love it.'

★

Many people in recent years have done a double-take on seeing press or TV coverage of a Thai boxing champion, for that same martial arts expert was also twice the champion dancer at Wigan Casino!

Sandy Holt's back-drops, spins and splits won him first place in the Casino's dance competition nearly twenty years ago. And that same agility and athleticism also brought him two national and one European Thai boxing titles.

Now in his late thirties, Sandy boasts that he can still fit into the 28in-waist baggy pants that he wore at his first dancing competition. And he has still got the leather brogues that helped him on his way. His affection for the Casino and the years he spent out on the floor is still apparent: 'They were the best years

Northern Noise

NUMBER 1

40p

SPECIAL TRIBUTE TO SIX INCREDIBLE·YEARS AT WIGAN CASINO

Plus THE MOD REVIVAL - WHERE WILL IT END?

PLUS LOTS MORE INSIDE

WIGAN CASINO No. 1

THREE TIMES OVER!

TOP ALLNIGHTER (Current)	ALL-TIME ALLNIGHTER	TOP OVERALL VENUE
1) **WIGAN CASINO**	1) **WIGAN CASINO**	1) **WIGAN CASINO**
2) ST. IVES	2) TORCH - STOKE	2) BLACKPOOL MECCA
3) NOTTS PALAIS	3) TWISTED WHEEL	3) NOTTS PALAIS

TOP ALLDAYER (All-time)

1) **RITZ - MANCHESTER**
2) CATS WHISKERS - BURNLEY
3) NOTTS PALAIS

TOP NORTHERN LABEL

1) **MOTOWN**
2) ATLANTIC
3) GRAPEVINE
4) CASINO CLASSICS

TOP ALL-TIME SINGLE

1) **DO I LOVE YOU**
2) OUT ON THE FLOOR
3) TIME WILL PASS YOU BY
4) WHAT
5) SWEETEST FEELING

of my life. It is a time I will never ever forget.'

Sandy was seventeen when he first went to the Casino. He bought a ticket for the first anniversary night in September 1974, but couldn't make it. Instead he went the following week and so started an obsession with dancing and the music that he cherishes to this day.

It was while watching the dancing competition at the second anniversary night that he decided he wanted to be the best. Said Sandy, who lives in Bolton: 'I was watching this guy who won the competition and he was really good, doing brilliant, really fast spins, and I thought: "That's what I want to do. I want to win that." But I knew I would need more practice before I was that good.'

So he went away and practised, and his martial arts training and stretching complemented his gymnastic dancing style. The following year he took part in the dancing contest – and won. He also got to the semifinals at the fourth anniversary and won the title again at the fifth.

Sandy recalled: 'Dancing was the main attraction for me. I used to dance literally all night. Some people travelled there just for the atmosphere, some just for the music and some just to dance. That was me. I was one of the very few who would dance all night and I did it without drugs. Some people did take drugs, and I can understand it. If they had travelled three or four hours to get there, the last thing they wanted to do was fall asleep. But I never took drugs. I was fit and I was into martial arts even then. A lot of the moves I did were martial arts moves.'

Sandy even managed a couple of hours' sleep before he set off for the all-nighters. He was usually in work at Warburton's bread factory at 6am on a Saturday and by teatime he was feeling tired. So he went to bed for two or three hours, stretched and set off for his dance marathon.

During his Casino fame he found himself featured in the *Sun* as the 'John Travolta of Wigan Casino' (John Travolta looked like a geriatric morris dancer compared to this guy!) and also danced for the cameras for a couple of TV programmes on Northern Soul.

'I was well into dancing and I was torn between professional dancing and doing martial arts. When the soul scene started to diminish I realized that there might not be a future in dancing so I chose martial arts.'

A wise move, as it turned out, for Sandy won major fight belts and now instructs in Thai boxing, with his own gyms in Bolton and Wigan. But even now he is still recognized by former Casino-goers as he travels around England and Scotland. In Aberdeen he met a guy who said he had turned up to a martial arts lesson because he remembered him from the Casino.

Sandy attends the occasional soul night now, but not as often as he would like – a far cry from his teenage years when he went to soul nights six nights a week.

'I suppose it was an obsession, but people have obsessions now. The rave scene of today is parallel to Northern Soul. I still have my original Casino membership card and all my records. I never get tired of them. The Casino was a phenomenon and I'll never forget my nights there.'

Part IV

The Beginning of the End

9

Tears, Nothing but Tears

Sooner or later it had to end. Nothing lasts for ever, but when that end came and the famous 'Three Before Eight' echoed across the packed, emotional dancefloor for the last time, it left a void in the lives of all concerned.

The warning signs had been there for a few years. Not because of drugs, not because of any suggestion of poor management or any other problems associated with the club, but simply because the local council wanted the land on which the Casino stood.

The Station Road site was owned by Wigan Council. Gerry Marshall owned the Casino building and leased the land from the council. Even in 1978, three years before the club's demise, Gerry became aware that the site would be needed one day for an extension of Wigan Council's civic centre. No definite date was fixed and, as far as anyone was aware, nothing was put in writing.

The following year, Gerry again mentioned to Russ that the council had been talking to him about the Casino site. The news cast a shadow over the future of the all-nighters, still at their peak, but management and staff carried on regardless in the hope that nothing would happen.

Gerry was understandably reluctant during that period to spend money on repairs if the club had an uncertain future, so some things weren't looked after, but for Northern Soul fans this just added to the unique appeal of the venue. So what if the toilets leaked and the carpets and walls were grubby? This was a

WIGAN CASINO SOUL CLUB IS CLOSING DOWN

WE NEVER REALLY HOPED TO HAVE TO ANNOUNCE THIS BUT DUE
TO NOT BEING ABLE TO NEGOTIATE A LONG ENOUGH LEASE AND
THE EFFECTS OF THE RECESSION, UNFORTUNATLEY IT IS
INEVITABLE.
MANY, MANY THANKS FOR YOUR MARVELLOUS AND SUCH LOYAL
SUPPORT IT REALLY IS A TEARFULL END FOR A WONDERFUL EIGHT
YEAR ERA SPREADING THE FAITH OF NORTHERN SOUL - WE'LL
NEVER FORGET YOU - WE HOPE YOU'LL NEVER FORGET US.

Russ Winstanley.

To Wigan Casino, Station Rd., Wigan, Lancs.
Friday Sept. 4th. LAST OLDIES NIGHTER
Please rush me...............TICKET(S) at £4.00 Each.
I enclose S.A.E. and P.O. for £..........

SATURDAY 19th. LAST NIGHTER
Please rush me...............TICKET(S) at £5.00 Each.
I enclose S.A.E. and P.O. for £..........

NAME.. TEL. No......................

ADDRESS...

....

....

....

Northern Soul all-nighter, a largely working-class, grass-roots music scene, not a trendy *Saturday Night Fever*-style disco with flashing lights, chicken in a basket and wine by the bottle.

The rumours of an imminent closure resurfaced again in 1980, and in the spring of 1981 Russ got the phone call that he had always dreaded. Gerry Marshall asked to meet him, and when Russ arrived he broke the news that the Casino would have to close later that year.

Russ, as the founder of the all-nighters and one of the prime movers behind the Casino's success, was devastated: 'I remember Gerry Marshall telling me: "That's it this time." I drove home with tears streaming down my face.'

The date set for the Casino's demolition meant that the club would probably have to close around September 1981. Instead of celebrating its eighth anniversary, the club would be staging a wake.

The farewell all-nighter was pencilled in for 19 September. Tickets at £5 each went on sale with this message from Russ: 'Many, many thanks for your marvellous and loyal support. It really is a tearful end for a wonderful eight-year era spreading the faith of Northern Soul. We'll never forget you. We hope you'll never forget us.'

The event was to run from midnight to 9am with DJ's Russ Winstanley, Richard Searling, Keith Minshull, Dave Evison, Brian Rae, Pat Brady and Gary Rushbrooke. Spinning the oldies in Mr M's were Kenny Spence, Stuart Brackenbridge, Steve Whittle and Brian Rae. It was bound to be an emotional send-off for one of the most famous clubs in British history.

Gerry, meanwhile, made arrangements to wind up Wigan Casino Ltd and started to make plans for his new Wigan venue, the Riverside Club.

Former Casino regulars set off from all corners of the UK on 19 September with mixed emotions. There could be no doubting that a memorable night lay ahead, but any elation was tinged with sadness that they would never again walk through those famous doors in Station Road.

It had been a long journey from those early days to the end of

WIGAN CASINO SOUL CLUB
SATURDAY, SEPTEMBER 19th, 1981
12 Midnight to 9.00 a.m.

RETAIN THIS PORTION
FOR DRAW

0743

END OF AN ERA - LAST NIGHTER
WITH THE COUNTRY'S No. 1 SOUL SPINNERS
RUSS, RICHARD, KEITH, DAVE, BRIAN, PAT, GARY, KENNY, STUART & STE

9 NON-STOP HOURS ON TWO FLOORS
FREE DRAW AT 3.30 a.m.
FOR MUSIC CENTRE - T.V.'s, RADIOS, ETC.
FINAL OF DANCE COMPETITION
1st Prize - £100, 2nd Prize - £75, 3rd Prize - £25

EVERYONE WILL RECEIVE
A FREE BADGE AND
SOUVENIR POSTER

OLDIES ALL-NIGHT IN
Mr. M's WITH
KENNY, STUART, STE &
BRIAN

Tickets £5.00 each Members Only
*Britain's Top D.J.'s, Management and Staff say goodbye to the
Best Ever Venue and Most Loyal Supporters*
THANKS FOR EIGHT INCREDIBLE YEARS

an era. Since 1973, many soul fans had left the scene, some never to return. Vast numbers had joined the Casino's legion of fans. Couples who started going as boyfriend and girlfriend were now man and wife. DJs had left and DJs had joined the famous line-up for the 12 till 8 shift.

Edward Heath was Prime Minister no more. Maggie Thatcher and the mass unemployment of the early 1980s were a fact of life. Wigan Casino badges were by now considered pretty naff by most soul fans, and ridiculously wide flares had given way to narrow-bottomed jeans and trousers. But even though times and fashions had changed, the Casino-goers' passion for the music and lifestyle of Northern Soul remained undiminished.

That much was obvious at the 'farewell' all-nighter. The dancefloors in the main hall and Mr M's were so packed it was a struggle to find any space virtually all night. The atmosphere was even more electric than usual and parting thank-yous from DJs as they finished their final spots at the doomed venue added

WIGAN CASINO NEWS

SEPTEMBER 19th, 1981

Welcome to the Last Saturday Nighter

Due to the fantastic demand for tickets, and the fact that so many members have been unable to attend, we have managed to secure the Casino for just one more Oldies All-Nighter on

FRIDAY, OCTOBER 2nd, 12 Midnight to 8.00a.m.

We will be recording a Souvenir Album of the night featuring

TOMMY HUNT

DUE OUT AT CHRISTMAS

THIS WILL BE NORTHERN SOULS MOST HISTORICAL NIGHT

We also hope to announce details of our new venue
**Britain's best D.J. Line Up (exclusive to the Casino)
will be,
RUSS WINSTANLEY, KEITH MINSHULL, BRIAN RAE, DAVE
EVISON AND GARY RUSHBROOKE
In Mr. Ms: KENNY SPENCE, STUART BRACKENBRIDGE
and STE WHITTLE**

TICKETS ARE ON SALE TONIGHT
at Reception after 3.30a.m.

Don't Miss Out - Tickets are £3.00

poignancy to the evening.

'Thanks for being a great crowd.'

'Thanks for eight great years. You've been fantastic. Hope to see you all again.'

By 9am in the sauna-like heat and soccer-match atmosphere of the Casino there was still no sign of the crowd having had enough. It seemed as if everyone was staying (literally) 'to the death'.

Eventually the 'Three before Eight' was spun. The clapping and noise rose as 'Long After Tonight is All Over', 'Time Will Pass You By' and 'I'm on My Way' rang out.

Russ, fighting back tears, thanked the crowd for their loyal support and tried to say goodbye. But no one moved. There was a great roar and the whistling, stomping and chanting started again.

'MORE, MORE, MORE, MORE ...'

No one wanted the night to end. So on went the 'Three before Eight' once more, to the delight of the dancers. And again and again.

As each record was played, the steady handclap of 2,000 people was joined by the constant chant of 'MORE, MORE, MORE, MORE ...'

Finally the lights came on and people realized it really was over. It was now 9.30am and the dancing had gone on for nine and a half hours.

The emotion when the final 'Three before Eight' had been spun was gut-wrenching. Grown men had tears in their eyes, people hugged each other and it seemed that the stomping, clapping and cheering would never end. Everyone who was there knew that their lives would somehow never be quite the same again.

Many fans arriving at the 'final' all-nighter had been astonished to find flyers advertising one more all-nighter. The Casino management had managed to secure the venue for another date, 2 October, and justified this surprise development by saying that the September one was a sell-out, that people had been disappointed not to get tickets, etc.

But many soul fans and observers saw it as a crafty way to make more money out of the club's demise. Russ, however, refutes this claim and explains that the extra oldies night arose because the council informed the Casino very late in the day that they would not need the site immediately. The Casino Company, under Gerry Marshall, had been wound up with the September final date in mind. So Russ and the then manager, Harry Green, took over the club for the 2 October all-nighter. Again there was a capacity crowd and another chance for the people to have a final fling. But inevitably there was a backlash, as some soul fans felt they were being taken for a ride.

The Casino stood idle and empty for another two months, until Russ and Harry staged another 'final' night on 6 December. This time the attendance was lower and the club was visibly deteriorating. It was a sad end to the Casino success story.

For Russ: 'I can understand why people didn't agree with what we did and we did get some flak – mainly from people who were running rival soul nights. I only wish we could have gone on for another twelve months. The council did nothing with the building and they lost another year's rent and rates, and we lost another year's enjoyment. The place just went to rack and ruin. It was awful to see the Casino go like that.'

One man who did not agree with the 'final nights' saga was Casino DJ Dave Evison. He remembers with sorrow searching for a copy of Jimmy Radcliffe's 'Long After Tonight is All Over' to play out the 'Three before Eight' at the September farewell all-nighter. He found one – just. 'I didn't agree with the way the Casino announced another "final" all-nighter when everyone arrived for what was supposed to be the last all-nighter. It was a pity because it meant that the place was only three-quarters full when it finally closed.'

Dave's fellow oldies DJ Steve Whittle, who played the last-ever record ('The Night') in Mr M's, agreed: 'It should have ended in September like it was supposed to do. I felt it was sad that they tried to squeeze another one or two all-nighters out of it. A lot of people who had supported the Casino over the last eight years felt conned. Don't get me wrong, the last night in December was a great night, but I feel the last one should have been the one in September.'

Dave summed up the success of Wigan thus: 'It was the right place at the right time and it hit all the right criteria. The Wheel and the Torch had built up the Northern Soul scene and it had to happen, and Wigan was there. All good things come to an end and the Casino had a damned good innings.'

In March 1982 the demolition of the Casino was hastened by a fire which broke out in the empty building, causing major damage to the offices, dancefloor and part of the roof. Within minutes of the alarm being raised, ten fire engines were at the scene, including crews from Bolton and Merseyside. It took more than an hour to bring the blaze under control. A fire brigade spokesman said the incident would probably mean the demolition order would be speeded up, but it was February 1983 before work got under way in earnest. Within a few days the hallowed site, which had been variously a garage, a concert venue and the home of Northern Soul was razed to the ground.

The *Wigan Observer* paid tribute to the Casino in a farewell article as the demolition contractors got to work. Under the headline 'Memories are Made of This', the local weekly paper reported:

For fifty years Wigan's Empress Ballroom (later the Casino) was the busiest night-spot in town. Now the once-crowded dance palace is just a ruined shell. The last strident notes of jazz, swing and pop discs have long since faded and its maple floor is now a ragged jumble of broken timbers and steel.

Open to the sky, the huge hall is almost unrecognizable as the venue for the stately ball, the regular Saturday hop and, in later years, the wilder gyrations of all-nighters.

Several generations of Wigan folk first took to the floor at the Emp, which opened on 1 November 1916. It was opened under the title of the Empress Hall and Garage. The ground floor was then a working garage.

Later the garage became a billiards hall and, still later, a café.

Its maplewood floor on steel springs had room for 350 dancers and the whole hall would seat 2,000. It had a spare room and kitchen. Over the decades the Emp was used for a variety of purposes: roller-skating, wrestling matches and other events were held there, as well as parties for poor children before the Second World War.

But it was during the last war and just afterwards that the old Emp entered its heyday, still in the hands of the Atherton family. The Emp bands were good, and there were several after Harry Atherton, including the big name Billy Forrest Orchestra, and there was singer Betty Corcoran, who was one of the all-time favourite vocalists there.

The Emp certainly evokes memories among people a generation or even two ahead of the youngsters who never knew it as anything other than the venue of the greatest Northern Soul all-nighters in history.

The week after that article appeared in the *Observer*, local folk shared their recollections of the sadly missed club. As E. Sixmith of Wigan wrote:

The very name the Emp brings back to me the times of the late 40s and early 50s. Big band swing, jiving, drape suits, DA haircuts, and going up the Emp every Monday and Saturday.

What a great time we had. Never to be forgotten. So it's goodbye at last to the good old Emp. You did a good job.

Another letter, signed A. Brigadier, recounted:

The first time I set foot in the place it was with a 10 shilling ticket purchased from the Empress Café as a surprise for me. I think that would be around 1963. The Rolling Stones were the group, I think, and I have memories of a packed hall, girls fainting, Brian Jones and a strange music the likes of which I had never heard before.

It was all played fast and very loud. I recall Manfred Mann a short time later, with Paul Jones singing 'Hootchie Cootchie Man' standing on top of the piano, much to the management's disapproval. I had a short conversation with David Bowie in the gents' toilet in the Palais de Danse. He was appearing with Long John Baldrie.

Herman's Hermits every Monday. They had a residence for a few weeks at the Emp until they recorded 'I'm into Something Good'. There was also Kingsize Taylor and the Dominoes on Monday in place of Herman's Hermits – he was the man who recorded the Beatles live in Hamburg.

And what of the council's extended civic centre, the reason they needed the site? It was never built.

Russ is understandably furious at that outcome: 'The members of Wigan Council need their heads examining for demolishing such a popular and multi-functional building. After numerous offers to take over the lease and even rebuild the club, their insurance company demolished it free of charge. Then the council said they had made a little mistake! They hadn't enough money left to extend the civic centre. The Casino need not have been knocked down. We had lost our home, our spiritual being, the world's most famous disco, and thousands of friends, and it need not have happened. What an absolute disgrace!'

A supermarket was built on the site, then it became a Job Centre and now the famous Station Road ground lies empty once more. A multistorey car-park occupies part of what used to be the Casino's car park across the road. But some things never die and eagle-eyed former regulars might well find it amusing to wander along at the rear of the site to spot the original doorway to Mr M's. A doorway to the past, indeed.

Russ was understandably devastated by the Casino's closure

and lost interest in the Northern Soul scene for many years. But he can proudly reflect on his role in the world's most famous club of its era: 'It was the right thing at the right time. We put Northern Soul in fashion. When the Casino closed it left a massive hole for me. But at least it went out at the top.'

10

Long After Tonight is All Over

Northern Soul refused to lie down and die after the Casino's closure and is still very much alive and kicking in these rave-dominated times. Although a major body-blow to the soul scene, Wigan's demise heralded the start of a new era and a new-look and more mature Northern Soul scene has emerged.

Critics of the Casino – often rivals jealous of its continued success – secretly welcomed its end. There had been mutterings for some time, with some justification, that Wigan's leaning towards oldies had led to its living in a timewarp. The country was full of entrepreneurs who thought, mainly wrongly, that they could do it better and maybe even as successfully as the Casino.

The reality of the situation was that for many soul fans the Casino was the ultimate venue, and during its lifetime they may have visited few if any other all-nighters. The Casino's demise was by design or accident the cue for many all-nighter-goers to 'retire' from the scene, either immediately or within the next few years. Many Casino-goers were in their mid- to late twenties, when engagement, marriage or parenthood beckons. The rebellious teenage years were passing for many and Northern Soul fans were getting ready to settle down and lead more 'normal' lives.

A lifestyle which included travelling the length of the country, staying out all night and arriving home hollow-eyed the next afternoon only to disappear to bed was not for many a recipe for domestic harmony if only one partner was into the music. If a couple were both Northern Soul fans there was the prospect of children, a lack of money and baby-sitters to worry about.

But for thousands of Northern Soul fans, their love of attending all-night or all-day events drove them to seek out new venues. Various events came and went, usually carrying the tag of 'Wigan revivals', and only a few became established favourites. Some forward-thinking DJs and promoters looked at Wigan's oldies-dominated play-lists and did the exact opposite by concentrating almost exclusively on newies. Others went for a mix of oldies and newies, and those who wanted to perpetuate the memory of the Casino kept paying homage with all-oldies revival nights.

Dave Evison, still a regular all-nighter DJ, said: 'Oldies have killed the scene in a way, but they are also responsible for saving it. It saved the scene but it destroyed Wigan. After Wigan closed, the die-hards refused to let the scene die. The reason that it's surviving at the moment is because of oldies – and that's because there is no new blood coming on to the scene. Only about 2 per cent are aged eighteen to twenty, everyone else is much older. Most other scenes come and go, but we've been here for nearly thirty years. The punters on the rave scene aren't really interested in the music but Northern Soul revolves around the records and collecting and always will.'

Some of the more successful early 1980s venues included Morecambe run by Shaun Gibbons, Clifton Hall at Rotherham, and the Top of the World at Stafford. That decade also saw the launch of an all-nighter which survives to this day: the 100 Club in London.

The Oxford Street club, well known as a jazz venue, is a relatively small event as it holds only around 300 people, but it has a reputation for quality soul music, an innovative music policy and enough pulling power to bring the crowds down to the capital from all over England.

As the venue prepares to celebrate its seventeenth

GROOVESVILLE SOUL PROMOTION

PRESENTS THE 1ST

NORTHERN SOUL AND MOTOWN ALL-NIGHTER

SATURDAY 14th DECEMBER 1991

AT

THE PIT

CNR DRUITT & SUSSEX STS

SYDNEY

11.00pm til 6.00am

$6.00 ADMISSION

SPECIAL GUEST DJ'S FROM THE U.K.

VINCE PEACH • FRANK DRISCOLL • DAVID MILTON • ROB MILTON • • FROM OZ AGENT 00 SOUL •

THE FIRST FULL SCALE ALL - NIGHTER EVER HELD IN AUSTRALIA FEATURING LEGENDARY NAMES LIKE: MAXINE BROWN, JACKIE WILSON, THE MONCLAIRS CHUCK JACKSON & GENE CHANDLER, AND CLASSICS LIKE: "CHANGE YOUR WAYS" "LANDSLIDE", "CONDITION RED", "IF THAT'S WHAT YOU WANTED", "LAST MINUTE MIRACLE", "SKIING IN THE SNOW" etc.

TICKETS AVAILABLE FROM GOOD GROOVE RECORDS

350 CROWN ST. DARLINGHURST (TEL: 331 - 2942) OR AT

THE DOOR. PLEASE NOTE THAT CAPACITY IS LIMITED

AND PREFERENCE WILL BE GIVEN TO TICKET HOLDERS

Groovesville Soul Promotions Presents the 5th

NORTHERN SOUL

AND

MOTOWN

ALLNIGHTER

Dance all night to rare soul classics from the 60's and 70's by Billy Butler, the Isley Brothers, Maxine Brown, The O'Jays, Gloria Jones, The Marvelettes, Jimmy Radcliffe, Mary Love and a cast of thousands spun by DJ's Agent Double-O-Soul and Vince Peach (ex Twisted Wheel and Wigan Casino)

**plus Motown record giveaways courtesy of Polygram records !
and Shindig video giveaways courtesy of Festival records !
and Rare 60's and 70's soul videos on screen !**

Sat 6th February 1993
10PM - 6AM
SIGHT NIGHTCLUB
171 Victoria St. Kings Cross.
Sydney (Ph. 358 4221)

$6 at the door
(be early - full house expected)

SOUL PROMOTIONS PROUDLY PRESENTS

OUR NEXT

Oldies All-Nighter

at the

CENTRAL PIER, MORECAMBE
27th MAY, 1983   11p.m. - 9a.m.

Regular Oldies All-Nighter fourth Friday of every month

Star D.J.'s in the Main Hall	In the Starlight Room spinning those Mr. M's memories
RUSS WINSTANLEY	STEVE WHITTLE
RICHARD SEARLING	RICHARD SEARLING
SHAUN GIBBONS	DEREK SMITH
BRIAN RAE	SHAUN GIBBONS
GARY RUSHBROOKE	MARK FARLEY
KEITH MINSHELL	

FULLY LICENSED BAR TILL 2.00a.m.
ADMISSION FOR MEMBERS £2.00   GUESTS £3.00

Come and see the resemblence to Wigan Casino at the Central Pier, Morecambe
FOOD   • TWO ROOMS • BALCONIES • ORIGINAL D.J.'S • CLOAKROOM
• AND THAT SPECIAL WIGAN SOUND •

"THE NEAREST THING TO THE CASINO YET"

COACH ORGANISERS TEL. LANCASTER 39230

TO ALL SOUL FANS WHO ATTENDED THE FIRST OLDIES ALL-NIGHTER
AT THE PIER LAST MONTH.
A **BIG THANKS** FOR MAKING IT A FANTASTIC NIGHTER AND A FABULOUS SUCCESS!!!
SEE YOU ALL ON THE 27th MAY.   MORECAMBE ALL-NIGHTERS ARE HERE TO STAY!

SEND FOR "FREE" LIFE MEMBERSHIP NOW AND SAVE A £1.00 ON THE NIGHT

- -

I AM OVER 18 YEARS OF AGE. PLEASE SEND ME A MEMBERSHIP FOR SOUL PROMOTIONS
Name...
Address..

Send S.A.E. to: SOUL PROMOTIONS, Central Pier, Marine Road, Morecambe, Lancs.
PROBABLY THE BEST ALL-NIGHTER IN THE WORLD!

THE COUNTRY'S BIGGEST NORTHERN SOUL ALL-NIGHTER

"THE RITZ"

MANCHESTER
WHITWORTH STREET (WEST)
EASTER SUN/MON 7/8TH APRIL 1995

RETURN OF THE ULTRA RARE NIGHT
12.00 MIDNIGHT TILL 8-00AM

ADM £7 MEMBERS

8 HOURS OF 100% CLASSIC SOUL MUSIC BROUGHT TO YOU BY THE NATIONS TOP DJ'S

E 4TH **6t's**

RTHERN SOUL WEEKENDER

ASSOCIATION WITH KENT RECORDS UK , PRESENT

DANCE DANCE DANCE

Featuring Non-Stop Stompers, Floaters, Oldies, Newies, Ancient and Modern, Out-A-Site Soul Records played by the Best Northern DJ's Around

AT THE BEACHOLME HOLIDAY CENTRE, NORTH SEA LANE

CLEETHORPES

Friday 7th-Sunday 9th June '96

DJ's include: Richard Searling, Butch, Pat Brady, Ginger, Mark Bicknell, Brian Rae, Mick Smith, Roger Banks, Ady Croasdell, Ian Clark, Keith Minshull, Jim, Saus, Guy Hennigan, Bob Hinsley, Andy Rix and Mighty BUB!
PLUS: the happening 70's /crossover suite, Richard , Terry Jones, Andy Davies, Cliff Steel, Adam, Ian Clark and Dave Thorley.

3 FULL NIGHTS AND DAYS FOR ONLY £44-£49 (INCLUDING TWO ALL-NIGHT SESSIONS)

Alternatively, Evening passes are available at, £10 Friday, £15 Sat. £10 Sun. Available ON THE DOOR.

HURRY THIS IS YOUR LAST CHANCE TO BOOK BY CALLING OUR BOOKING HOTLINE

TEL: 01858 465780 OR
FAX: 01858 468020

NOW!

anniversary, organizers have seen not only many old faces flocking back to the scene but lots of new ones. Suddenly Northern Soul is back in fashion in the capital.

The man behind the 100 Club is Ady Croasdell, alias Kent Records, prolific producers of Northern Soul albums and CDs: 'It started off basically as a reaction to Wigan. We felt that Wigan had got all very "poppy", so we wanted to get back to the roots and play more classic early 60s sound that didn't have to have a 100mph beat. Mid-tempo stuff like Bobby Bland, Maxine Brown, the Impressions, and it didn't have to be rare, either.'

The play-list leans heavily on 'new' discoveries and the monthly all-nighters have attracted a strong following from the South, although more Northerners have attended as the 100 Club's reputation has spread.

Said Ady: 'The Northern Soul scene never went away for us, because we have been here since Wigan's days. There was a period in the 80s and the early 90s when it was harder, but we have had a good revival in the last two years. The North has had a different kind of revival from older people coming back after their kids have grown up and that kind of thing. Down here the crowd is generally new and Northern Soul is a buzz word again, something to drop into a conversation. It's very fashionable and everyone wants to know at the moment. Even the guys from Oasis and Primal Scream have popped in to see what it's all about.'

So will the 100 Club all-nighters still be going into the twenty-first century with Mr Croasdell behind the decks?

According to Ady: 'I can certainly see it going for another ten years, and after that we will have to see. I'm very happy that people are still going to all-nighters, but I have been doing this for so many years I'm quite knackered. I would rather be doing early evening dances and going home drunk at 2am!'

The relentless search for rarities and the business skills of people like Ady have led in the 1990s to priceless unissued recordings for American labels being accessible to all. And CD compilations using master tapes and digital recordings have improved not only the sound quality but the availability of rare sounds which in the Casino's day would have cost you your mortgage.

Soul fans buying the latest CD for about £13 are getting a collection of tracks which on the original labels would set them back hundreds of pounds. All-nighters in the 1970s were packed with record dealers selling vinyl. Now those dealers and collectors are competing for space with others selling massive selections of Northern Soul CD compilations, many of which contain detailed sleeve notes and photos from great venues.

Goldmine's *Wigan Casino Story* has proved a best-seller, as well as its *Twisted Wheel Story, The Golden Torch Story* and *The Blackpool Mecca Story*.

Another moderately sized venue is Tony's Empress Ballroom in Blackburn, where the monthly all-nighters have been running successfully now for five years.

For many people the leading all-nighters in Britain are now Keele University and the Ritz in Manchester. Each venue turns its attention to Northern Soul only about four times a year, but when it does more than 1,000 souls pack it out.

Keele consists of a massive dancefloor, record bar and bar areas, and the atmosphere and crowd are reminiscent of the Casino – except that some dancers weren't even born when the Casino opened, and the others are a little greyer or heavier! Its 10pm to 8am sessions have now been running for eight years, and organizer Neil Clowes wants to beat Wigan by reaching the ninth anniversary. A well-run venue on a self-contained university site with plenty of parking, there is no reason to presume Keele will not achieve its goal.

The Ritz in Manchester was well known as an all-day venue in the 1970s. Its famous raised 'bouncy' dancefloor has been brought down to ground level. But the dancing area is still large, with a balcony above from where soul fans can relax or watch the gyrations below. And when you stand with hundreds of others outside the Ritz at midnight waiting for the doors to open, it is easy to recapture the same sense of anticipation that hit you outside a certain club in Wigan twenty years earlier.

Run by former Wigan Casino DJ Richard Searling, who also has a Sunday afternoon show on Jazz FM in Manchester, you will find a lot of familiar Casino faces there. Dave Evison, Soul Sam, Kev Roberts and Chris King all make regular guest appearances behind the decks.

The Northern Soul scene has matured, along with many of its followers. The tempo of the music is often a little slower, and beat ballads of the 1960s which would have been considered 'too slow' at Wigan are now a big feature.

The current resurgence in popularity of Northern Soul has led to the launch of an increasingly popular fanzine called *Manifesto*. In 1994 the Gloucester-based publication, run by Ian Palmer and Dennis Lee, started out with the aim of providing what had been lacking in soul fanzines – a sense of fun and chat about the regular faces on the scene.

Said Ian: 'There were fanzines around that gave detailed record listings and reviews of the latest CDs, which were fine for the real enthusiast, but there was nothing that covered the social scene. There are so many crazy characters about and many people just want to go out and have a good laugh. The Northern scene isn't just about a load of anoraks sitting around talking about matrix stamps and record labels. There is another side to it and we wanted to get people excited about going out to venues again.'

Manifesto is now on sale at most venues and by mail order, and Ian and Dennis have subscribers as far away as Australia, Malaysia, Japan, America, Canada, and most of Europe. And not all of them are Brits who have ventured abroad.

Ian again: 'An Austrian guy rang me the other day because he wanted some magazines to sell in his shop. I gather that Germany are holding all-nighters, and they are trying to get them going in Perth. A guy from the States rang up to say he had just been to an all-nighter in San José. They probably run them differently to us but they still play what we would call Northern Soul.'

Like many people, Ian had a break from the soul scene in the early 1980s, after Wigan's demise, but got his interest back about five or six years ago. After a few local soul nights he went to the Ritz all-nighter; 'I was knocked out to see so many people there and to see what a lot of enthusiasm everyone still had for the music. That got me back into it and I'm probably having more fun now than I was when I was a teenager. There are quite a few new faces coming to all-nighters now, but not as many as we would like. A lot of the crowd have been around for years. The problem is, and Wigan was a classic example, that when it becomes full of new faces the old regulars start slagging the place off. They feel that their territory is being encroached upon. But without the new faces the scene would have ground to a halt.'

Like many soul fans, Russ found the period immediately after the Casino's closure an anticlimax. He DJed at the successful Morecambe all-nighters and other venues, but found his interest waning.

He moved on to other things, but inevitably the pull of the music proved too strong in the 1990s. Now he is enjoying the revival and is DJing again at various venues, enjoying the 'second coming' of Northern Soul.

Russ said: 'When the Casino closed it just left a massive hole for me. I started to lose interest. I tried to break away, but as everyone knows, if it is in your blood you can't stay away from the music for too long.'

Outsiders may find it odd that people in their thirties and forties are reliving a scene that others thought had died in the 1970s. But like former Casino guest DJ Pep says, Northern Soul is a passion. He is still very active on the scene, particularly in his home base of the West Midlands. He said: 'In some respects Northern Soul has never been away, but there are a large number of people who have come back on board in recent years. People had a chance to get off the train to bring up a family or whatever and now they are getting back on it again fifteen to twenty years later. It's nice to be able to do that and it doesn't look like Northern Soul is going away. It's too much of an obsession.'

Blackburn all-nighter promoter Little Scotty ('don't print my real name or no one will recognize me') said: 'The revival that Northern Soul is going through at the moment is unbelievable. You can go to soul and Motown nights in the Wolverhampton area now and there are 300 to 400 people in all sweating like mad on the dancefloor. They are all thirty-odd and forty plus. The heart-attack rate will be up by another 50 per cent in five years' time at this rate!'

Scotty's Blackburn venue prides itself on being a medium-sized dancehall where everyone knows everyone else. And there are no DJs with egos playing to empty dancefloors, just the sounds old and new that the punters demand.

'Blackburn tends to be a big happy family. It's enjoyable soulful and friendly,' said Scotty. 'The all-nighter which brings back the most memories of Wigan for me is Keele. The atmosphere and the venue is unbelievable. I also go to the 100 Club, Leeds, St Ives and other venues, so as a promoter no one can accuse me of not supporting other venues!'

As Russ has said: 'People are fitter, physically and mentally, than ever now. So why shouldn't they enjoy soul nights in their thirties and forties? Anyway, what's the alternative?'

The music, like the punters, has also matured. No one in their right mind would play 'Footsee', 'The Wigan Joker' or dozens of other Casino records these days, because the dancefloor would empty. Similarly, sounds which never took off at the Casino are now immensely popular. Ruby Andrews's 'Just Loving You' is one example of a record that used to get sent out in 'budget' soul packs because no one rated it. A mint copy would now be a very tidy investment. Then you have dozens of timeless classics like the Salvadors' 'Stick by Me, Baby' and Yvonne Baker's 'You Didn't Say a Word', which are still instantly recognized and loved by virtually everyone who ever went to the Casino.

Unreleased Motown material, Detroit unknowns and rediscovered oldies all make the Northern Soul scene of the 1990s an interesting place.

The crowd who maybe in the early 1980s got married, drifted

away or concentrated on their careers have now found an old friend in Northern Soul. Their children are growing up, many people are disenchanted with the bland pop music of the 1990s and even children 'force-fed' Northern Soul by their parents are now old enough to be curious for themselves.

Young people fed up with the rave scene are now finding that Northern Soul offers them more diverse sounds and an adult scene that puts the music and friendship first.

Former Casino DJ Steve Whittle hopes the trend towards attracting younger people countinues: 'The rave scene today is basically just what we were doing twenty years ago. Staying up all night, travelling all over the country to sweaty clubs – apart from the music there's no difference. What disappoints me is that there are not as many young people on the scene as I would like. It has been a problem for fifteen years, and with the average age of soul fans about the mid-thirties in ten or fifteen years it will be like an old age pensioners' scene! Once all the old faces have stopped going, we might not have a Northern Soul scene any more.'

Go to the annual Cleethorpes Northern Soul weekender and you might well find mum, dad and the kids enjoying a three-day marathon of music. More than 700 people attended the 1996 event and enjoyed three days and two all-night sessions. The event, again run by Ady Croasdell, brought soul fans from as far away as America, Austria, Germany and Spain.

Magazine, newspaper, TV and radio articles on the 1990s Northern Soul scene are also awakening interest. Features in 1996 alone include trips by Radio 4 to the Blackburn all-nighter, Granada TV to the King George's Hall in Blackburn (with footage from the Casino), Radio 1 to the Cleethorpes weekender, and Channel 4 to Cleethorpes for their *Short Stories* programme.

DJ Mighty Bub said: 'Northern soul is the biggest underground scene in Britain. It has been for a long, long, time. We need new blood and as long as they come with the right attitude they are welcome.'

For Jeanette Flood from Dublin: 'Northern Soul is a

passion. It's the one thing that keeps me going through the week. Working in a crappy job and living on a housing estate, the only thing to do is to get away for weekends like this.'

Those words don't sound too dissimilar to those spoken by Dave Withers about Wigan Casino nearly twenty years earlier. So if you are approaching middle age, put the pipe and slippers on hold for a while and relive your misspent youth. Or, if you never went to the Casino, go to a Northern Soul venue and get an idea of what the fuss was all about.

There will *never* be another Wigan Casino. But the Northern Soul promoters of the 1990s are having a damned good try.

Part V

Afterthoughts

Visitors to the Casino could loosely be split into three main categories.

First, there was THE SOUL DEVOTEE: This was a staunch Northern Soul fanatic who would die without his weekly 'fix' of a Wigan Casino all-nighter. Possibly teetotal and would rather stay in than go out with his non-soul-loving mates to a 'normal' disco. Hates pop music, wouldn't dream of listening to Radio 1 or watching *Top of the Pops*, and spends all week waiting for Saturday night. Spends Sunday and the early part of the following week recovering from it. Lean, gaunt and athletic when the mood takes him. Phenomenal record collection all filed alphabetically in label order. Party trick is to recite serial numbers, B-sides, arrangers and producers of any given Northern Soul track. Spends almost nothing on clothes but spends hours putting knife-edge creases in his trusty jeans and T-shirts and polishes his brogues to a high sheen. Spouse/girlfriend/parents don't understand him and wonder when he'll 'grow out of it'. Searches high and low for soul night or all-dayer within 100-mile radius and sometimes combines them with an all-nighter to make it a 'proper weekend'. Looks permanently tired, eyes sunken and dark-ringed, but thinks he looks OK. Can't imagine life without Wigan Casino or a similarly 'hip' club.

Second, there was THE SOUL FAN. Regular visitor to the Casino and other clubs, but not as frequently as the devotee. Loves Northern Soul but not to the point of obsession. Probably likes other types of music – funk, disco, even rock – and spends many a night on the town with non-soul fans. Enjoys going to a pop disco and getting ratted and making a fool of him/herself dancing to old Tamla Motown records in Wigan style. Has a moderate record collection or gets mates to make up tapes. Thinks the Casino is wonderful but realizes there are other things in life. Doesn't take the whole scene too seriously. Misses all-nighters where necessary when nagged by spouse/girlfriend/parents.

And finally, THE TOURIST. Isn't really sure what the hell Wigan Casino is but everyone seems to think it's a cool place. Is it an all-night gambling den? May remember seeing something on the telly about it. Perhaps been dragged along by his mates, who have just started going. May like soul music or could just as easily be into Led Zeppelin, Elton John or the Osmonds. May have had a skinful en route to the all-nighter and in danger of curling up in a corner and going to sleep at 2am. Could be found under a pile of holdalls when the lights go on. Might hate the place and decide to go on to the dancefloor and take the piss out of the dancing style. Hurriedly changes mind after hard stares from large coloured gentleman. Might be bowled over by the place, make new friends and become a regular long after his mates have decided to move on to the next 'trendy' spot. Or could just walk around his local pubs wearing baggy pants adorned with Wigan Casino badges to 'impress' his younger mates into thinking he is one of the Casino 'faces'.

Which one were you?!?

Dave Nowell
of Blackpool

I was about fifteen and still at school in Chorley when I first heard about Wigan Casino. If someone had told me then what an influence that club would have on the rest of my life I would never have believed them.

I was a fairly late convert to soul music in some respects, having grown up listening to the Beatles, heavy rock groups like Deep Purple and Uriah Heep, and later David Bowie. Then in about 1973–4 I started to get more into commercial soul music like the Detroit Emeralds' 'Feel the Need in Me' and Barry White stuff.

The guys at school were by this time wandering around talking about Northern Soul instrumentals like 'Sliced Tomatoes' (Just Brothers) and 'Cigarette Ashes' (Jimmy Conwell). I wondered what the hell they were on about and showed no interest in Wigan Casino until early 1975. By then I had left school and there were various characters in the Chorley area already going to the all-nighters – Billy Vosper, Podge (Dave Frearson), Slim and other guys. Me and my mate Dave Lancaster from Burnley were by then going to the odd soul night in Burnley (the Rose Room and the Circulation Club), and elsewhere.

By the spring of 1975 I could not resist it any longer and asked my parents if I could go to the Casino all-nighter. The place already had a dubious reputation and so my dad asked a detective who lived nearby for his opinion of this strange club which was always in the newspapers and on the television.

The policeman described it as a 'den of iniquity' and I immediately thought, 'This sounds like my kind of place.' But my parents were having none of it and refused to let me go. A couple of months later, however, when I turned seventeen they reluctantly agreed.

So Dave Lancaster and I found ourselves on the last bus from Chorley to Wigan to await the doors opening at 2am for our first Casino all-nighter. That first visit was awe-inspiring. The heat, the atmosphere and the crowds were incredible. The music was weird and wonderful and totally unknown to us and the whole experience seemed unreal.

Betty Wright was on live that night and she just took the roof off the place with her performance. From that night on, my whole social life and music tastes changed, and over the next seven years I gained lifelong friends, great memories and a passion for the music that lives with me to this day.

The magic of the Casino was a combination of experiences: the anticipation on a Saturday morning, knowing that you wouldn't see your bed until maybe the next afternoon; phoning round friends to make arrangements; making an excuse to the girlfriend to take her home at 11pm instead of going to a nightclub; driving through the dark country lanes to Wigan with the cassette on and the car full of excited chatter; pulling into the packed car park and going in search of friends you perhaps hadn't seen for weeks or months.

It was the buzz you got from walking into the seething club and seeing the already-packed dancefloor; shouting so much over the music that come morning you were almost hoarse; feeling an incredible sensation of belonging when you hit the dancefloor; realizing that the hours were flying by and the rest of the world was asleep. Then there was the sense of shellshock when the lights went on at 8am and you had to re-enter the outside world: sitting muttering over a brew at Charnock Richard services or going back to a friend's house for several more hours of soul music or perhaps a lunchtime pint. It was having your head full of records, some that you couldn't name, that haunted you for the whole day afterwards; lying in bed in the afternoon reliving the all-nighter and finding that sleep wouldn't come.

It was all of these things and more. The Casino's friendliness was amazing. It was the only disco I ever went to alone without knowing that anyone I knew would be there. It literally did not matter if you wandered about the place all night on your own, chatting to various groups of people.

Strangers would quite often come up to you and ask for a fag or a swig of Coke and they were rarely refused. It was easy to get chatting to strangers and many firm friendships were formed. All the Casino-goers in Chorley, Leyland and Preston got to know one another and buses, cars and trains would be shared.

The Burnley crowd would know the Blackburn crowd, who knew the Bolton lot, who had friends among the Dundee crowd, who knew the Edinburgh and Falkirk mob, and so it went on.

The regular Saturday all-nighters became the focal point of my week, and were replaced some years later by the monthly oldies all-nighters, when other commitments made it difficult to attend more often.

I remember seeing Tommy Hunt at the second anniversary, Edwin Starr (brilliant, several times), Jackie Wilson (disappointing, but he was becoming ill), the Marvelettes, Martha Reeves, Billy Butler (he and the crowd got so bored he walked off early), Archie Bell and the Drells (I saw them a few hours later at the Ritz all-dayer too), the Chi-Lites, Gloria Jones and Junior Walker.

The best times for me were the late 70s and early 80s, when I had money to throw around in the record bar, a car and some great mates. Dave Ward from Leyland, Nick Varela from Blackburn, Noel Smith and Roger Wormald from Leyland, Mick Roberts and Co. from Chorley, the Horwich lot (Carole Thornley, Ste Livesey, Kev, etc.), the Falkirk mob (Jackie Pritchard, Tommy Cockburn, Hank, Una, Avron, Barbara and all the lassies), to name but a few.

The final nights at the Casino and the emotion as dancers

refused to move from the floor when the last records had been spun will live with me for ever.

I remember looking up at Russ Winstanley as he played 'Do I Love You?' over and over again and I swear he was crying. A Scots bloke I was standing with suddenly filled up and said: 'I can't stand it,' and walked out for the final time. Thanks, Wigan Casino, for a great youth.

Dave Lancaster of York
(formerly of Burnley)

My first visit to the club was to see Betty Wright. We sat in awe on the balcony – we couldn't believe the excitement, enthusiasm and sheer energy created by the place.

Betty was a brilliant performer and after everyone present had shown their appreciation the Northern beat began pounding again, accompanied by the regular clapping in perfect unison that was a trademark of our scene. We sat there tentatively wondering how we could possibly fit in with so many expert dancers. I've never to this day seen as many good dancers as there were then – some who actually went on to become professional dancers started their careers here.

The spins they did were out of this world. I remember one guy, Sandy, who made the centre spread in the *Sun*. He was a bread delivery driver during the day but he was a frequent winner of the Casino's dance competitions. He had a punishing training regime which included 5-mile runs, gymnastics and kick-boxing.

I saw many class acts over the years. One of my favourites was the late great Jackie Wilson clad in a skin-tight brown leather suit, which made his emaciated body look even worse but it didn't affect his soulful voice. It was such a tragedy he died so young.

Another brilliant performer was Junior Walker. It was pure ecstasy listening to melodic saxophone. Martha Reeves and the Exciters were also good, to name but a few. I went to the Casino by train, bus and even hitched it from Aldershot once with an old Army buddy, Bob Burton from Richmond, near Catterick.

We initially hitched it to Burnley on Friday night to my mum's, went straight out to a nightclub, got legless and staggered home in the early hours. We managed to get a lift to Wigan on the Saturday night and it was a nice feeling to be walking among the crowds gathered outside, trying to make out friends past and present from every possible destination.

If it was raining we would make for the cinema across the road and shelter from the elements in the doorway. Once the Casino's doors opened it was everyone for himself as you struggled to get in en masse with your holdall poised above your head and clutching your membership card tightly.

During the early hours Bob disappeared and about an hour and a half later I went to investigate the toilets. On calling his name he shouted back, kicking open his door, and there he was, cool, calm and collected, sitting on the toilet sewing his Wigan badges on to his singlet (don't ask me where he got his needle and thread from).

Bob then requested a record for us both and Russ played a very apt one – 'You've Come a Long Way, Baby', Flower Shoppe. What a night! The next day a mate dropped us off at the sliproad for the M6 and looked on in disbelief as we headed off, penniless, to hitch it back to Aldershot.

The Casino was sheer escapism for thousands from the humdrum life of office jobs or monotonous factory work. In the morning we used to like having a stroll in the nearby park or unwinding in the pool at Wigan Baths. The Casino was as much a part of Wigan as Uncle Joe's Mint Balls or Wigan Pier.

Please let's have a revival so I can don my full-length leather, button-down Ben Sherman and Spencers soul bags!

Tim Ashibende
of Shelton, Stoke-on-Trent

I think anyone who went to Wigan Casino cannot help but feel it has left them with a legacy of something that's hard to pinpoint. When I start thinking for any length of time about Wigan Casino I become very emotional about it, because I loved it. It has made a deep impression on my life and left me with memories of good times and good people which will be with me for ever.

I went from 1975 to the day it closed, and missed very few nights in all those years. There will never be anything to match the Casino: it was the building itself, the location, the era, the music, the people, the smells and everything all rolled into one.

It can never be replicated; perhaps that's the sad part. You know it's gone for ever. There was a magic about it all which started with packing your holdall and making your way to Keele services, right through to sitting on Sandbach services the next day, which is hard to articulate.

Tim remembers only ever seeing two fights at the Casino. One concerned two characters posing as the drug squad who were 'confiscating' items from people. They were identified when the lights were switched on and not given too easy a time by angry punters. Another concerned two blokes in the record bar fighting in 1981 over a record deal struck at the Torch (which closed in 1973!).

Tim and the Stoke lads will also never forget the elderly glass collector. According to Tim: 'He wasn't a day under sixty and emaciated as hell. All the Stoke lads used to call him the Skull. He seemed so incongruous there and so impassive and oblivious in the face of all the frenzied activity around him.'

As for the characters Tim knew, who usually graced the 'Stoke Corner' on the left of the dancefloor, near the archway into the record bar, the list is endless: Dave Alcock, Andy Myatt, Dave Bell, Mickey 'Moonshine', Racker, Elaine Higginson, Christine Humphries, Billy Jackson, Doris and Annie, Sharron Pearce, Suzanne Bloor, Yvonne and Carolyn Megyesi, Pablo, Blondy, Butch, Pecker, Ian Plant, Ant Dobson, Skinner, Tommo, Jimmy Phillips, The Conno's, Ruscoe, Phil Oliver, Tina, Gally, Sutt, TD, Pipe, Flea, Ted, Bob McNicholl, Helen Coulton, Johnny F, Cos, Atlas, Jeff Oakes, Martin Meyler, Tony 'Cong', Jem Ashibende, Becko, Paddy, Wol and, of course, Keith 'The Minsh' Minshull and Dave Evison.

Others from Stoke who would have loved to see their names in such a book had they lived: Taz (Paul Taylor), Johnny 'Hodge' (Hodgkinson), Fester, Kenny Litherland, Shaun and Little Willie. And not forgetting friends from elsewhere: Lewi from Runcorn, Pete Widd from Southampton, Mick Smith, Ady Croasdell, Randy Couzens, Hovis, Rod Shard, Dave Withers, Rob Mariott, Gary and Julie Rushbrooke, Gaz Kellett, Tommo, Mud, Tony Warot, Kim and Dave, Pete Lawson, Guy Hennigan, Margaret, Steve Whittle, Budgie and Dave Greet.

Oh, and Tim's girlfriend Jacqui Kavanagh, who went to Wigan while a very young teenager.

Tim Ashibende of Shelton, Stoke

1. 'Nothing Can Compare to You' Velvet Satins
2. 'Baby, Without You' Danny Monday
3. 'Try a Little Harder' Keymen Strings
4. 'If You Ever Walked Out of My Life' Dena Barnes
5. 'You Don't Love Me' Epitome of Sound
6. 'Night Owl' Bobby Paris
7. 'My World is on Fire' Jimmy Mack
8. 'The Day My Heart Stood Still' Ollie Jackson

9. 'Sweet Magic' Servicemen
10. 'Too Much of a Good Thing' Ambassadors

Brian Goucher
of Sheldon, Birmingham

I spent seven of the best years of my life travelling from Birmingham to Wigan and the Mecca. I have very strong vivid memories of the Casino. I'm forty now and I have some 15,000–20,000 records. I still spend between £100 and £200 a month on soul music.

I never concentrated on one particular era, which caused some quite heated exchanges with 60s die-hards. Once Wigan and the Mecca closed their doors, I stopped going to soul clubs. There simply wasn't anywhere else to go.

Hanging in my record room is a black and white photograph of the front of the Casino, taken from the car park – without doubt one of my real possessions.

I couldn't give you a Top Ten sounds from Wigan – even now some of the cover-ups are turning up – but I will however choose two records that sum up my feelings about the Casino and the Mecca: from the Casino it has to be Mel Britt's 'She'll Come Running Back', on FIP. I've had some silly bids lately to get my copy off me – no chance. From the Mecca, Denise Keeble and 'Before It Falls Apart' on Pelican. What can I say?

Mike Cunningham
of Ashton-in-Makerfield, Wigan

I started going to the all-nighters in 1974 and even now remember them perfectly.

In 1975 I went to college in Plymouth and met up with a guy called Richard Greene from Nottingham (that's his real name, honest), who was also into Northern Soul. He used to go to Nottingham Palais. We managed to find a small soul club that would play our records as long as we took them along – the 150 Club over Jets disco on Union Street.

Through going to the 150 Club, we met a group of kids from Torpoint in Cornwall who were into Northern Soul and for the two years I was in Plymouth, 1975 to 1977, we hung around together. Our nearest Northern Soul club was the Blue Lagoon in Newquay, a round trip of just over 100 miles.

But of course we regularly went to the all-nighters at Wigan. This time the round trip was over 600 miles. Many of the records had stupid-sounding names by stupid-sounding groups. I remember one time going into Russ Winstanley's shop in Wallgate and asking if he had 'Inky Dinky Wang Dang Do' by the Dramatics. The whole shop, which was fairly full, cracked up laughing. I suppose it did sound funny – but I don't see how you can ask for that record without sounding a prat.

As for favourite sounds, my favourite was 'She'll Come Running Back' by Mel Britt, closely followed by 'Night Owl' by Bobby Parris. I'm a biker now – have been for years. I was a steward at two of the big Hells Angels rallies this year, but I still remember my roots and nothing moves me more than rhythm and blues.

Una Hanlon-Schafer
of Aberdeen (formerly of Bonnybridge)

Wigan Casino was a very important part of my life. One of my friends, Liz Ryan, told me about it. I was only seventeen then. A few weeks later in our local, the Metro, we were doing our basic 'shuffle' when a guy who was also shuffling introduced himself as Les Brown.

He asked if we would be interested in a trip down to Wigan as he and some friends were hiring a bus. So the following Saturday we were on our way. And so I met the rest of what was to become our crowd – Tommy, Hank and Les (Leggy) were old friends and were already regulars at the Casino. We were the newcomers – Jackie Pritchard, Avron Hamilton, Liz, Wendy Robertson and myself.

I'll never forget the feeling I had the first time I walked through the doors – the atmosphere was so brilliant you could almost cut it with a knife! The music echoing off the high ceiling, the dancers all facing the DJ, all dancing on their own, clapping their hands in unison at certain parts of a record.

The first half of the night I spent watching people dancing. I wasn't brave enough to hit the floor. Towards the end of the night, I had developed the beginning of my own individual footwork.

When it came to the end of the all-nighter and they all filed into the Beachcomber, I must admit I did think they were all mad. But needless to say after a few more trips I was never off the dancefloor either. Steve Allen, known as Sallie, from Eccles and his mate Marc were the first friends I met there. After a few months I had friends from all over – Dave, Loz, Tich, Mike and

Jonah from Manchester, Terry from Wrexham, a great crowd from Dudley.

My Dudley mates were Pete Ricketts, Brillo, Max, Winston. By this time we had a great network in Scotland. We would attend a different soul club every night. My only night in was a Tuesday. We went to Edinburgh, Stirling, our own night in Falkirk and all-nighters in Dundee and Edinburgh.

We all continued to hire minibuses, cars and even came in a lorry once. When Edwin Starr was on I was right at the front. When he threw his shirt into the crowd I caught it.

If I ever had any problems or felt under stress or anything, it was all forgotten as soon as I got to the Casino, just dancing and singing away to the music. So after Wigan being the centre of my life for five years, I went travelling with my friend Jean Duffy. When the very last all-nighter was on I was working in Holland.

We seriously considered flying over for the weekend but we couldn't make it. We met some people around the world who had been to Wigan. When we worked in Greece, a guy there went to Wigan, we met a Welsh guy in Singapore who used to go and someone stole all Jean's badges off her holdall in Singapore airport. And I did see in Sydney a poster for a dance night which listed Northern Soul!

Una Hanlon-Schafer of Aberdeen

1. 'Gonna be a Big Thing' Yum Yums
2. 'Moody Woman' Jerry Butler
3. 'This Gets to Me' Pookie Hudson
4. 'I Wanna Give You Tomorrow' Benny Troy
5. 'Don't Depend on Me' Fantastic Johnny C
6. 'My Sugar Baby' Connie Clark
7. 'They'll Never Know Why' Freddie Chevez
8. 'Better Use Your Head' Little Anthony and Imperials
9. 'Waterfall' Jimmy Cliffe
10. 'Send Him Back' Pointer Sisters

Elizabeth Burke
of St Annes, Lancashire

My eldest brother Tony Burke moved to Blackpool from Garstang in 1973 aged seventeen. When he came back to visit the family he would fetch his records, introducing my sister Angela and my three best friends, Judith Delves, Anne Chapman and Stephanie Orr, to Northern Soul.

That was it. We were hooked on the music and we would tape his records before he went back to Blackpool. In 1974 Judith, Angela and I, along with Tony, went to the Catholic Club, alias the Alexandra Hotel, in Lancaster, which played Northern Soul. There we first learned to dance to the music.

In the autumn of 1975 we found ourselves going on the bus with Tony and a Blackpool lad nicknamed Epic to Preston. There we caught the train to Wigan – we were on our way to the Casino. We were excited and nervous at the same time.

I couldn't get over the dancers – back-flips, back-drops, the splits and spins – what a brilliant sight. After that first night we tried to go every weekend. Sometimes we made a weekend of it, going to the Ritz all-dayers in Manchester. My favourite time there was seeing Edwin Starr on stage.

The family then moved to St Annes in 1976 and I quickly made friends with Cath Langley and Gill Smith, who, I discovered, were into the soul scene. Then we started going to Lytham Football Club with Jon Le Saint as DJ so we could go and listen to our music locally. I then met Mick Wilding and we moved into a flat together. Our flat was always full at the weekends. We'd go to Wigan and friends like Tim Wilson, Rob Laird, Dale Cowley, Tim Hart, all from Fleetwood, would come back and we would have a great time talking and playing our music.

The great thing is that we all keep in touch today. Lytham Lions Club is on every three months or so and the same people go today as did fifteen years ago. My favourites are 'I'm Coming Home in the Morning' (Lou Pride), 'One Hundred Pounds of Pain' (Lenny Welch), 'Keep on Keeping on' (Nole Porter), 'She's Looking Good' (Rodger Collins) 'Exodus' (Biddu Orchestra), and in fact anything that's got a good stomp in it.

Ian Curtis
of Broadway, Worcestershire

The feeling of actually getting into the Casino for the first time was summed up by Tommy Hunt when he performed there live.

In his rendition of 'Help Me Make It Through the Night' he changed the words to 'Cause tonight, at the Wigan Casino, I've found my friends', and that has always summed up the way I felt every time I went (which was very regular from the mid-70s to the last night).

I can also remember quite often, when I had got no transport, thumbing a lift from Worcester to Wigan for the all-nighters and was extremely grateful for the lifts I got from the public and future friends who were also going. The first record I could afford to buy was Bobby Parris's 'Night Owl' on Cameo from Russ Winstanley himself.

The furthest I had to travel to make sure that I didn't miss the all-nighters was Northern Ireland. I had gone on holiday with my future wife and in-laws for a fortnight to Melano by car. In the middle of the holiday I decided I couldn't miss the all-nighter, so on the Friday night I drove from Northern Ireland to Dublin and then by ferry to Holyhead and then on to Wigan for the Saturday all-nighter.

Afterwards we drove all the way back, arriving early Sunday evening, to be invited out to another ordinary disco (what a let-down), which I had to go to. I did enjoy the Casino, the music (and still do) and all the people, the new friends and the great entertainers who appeared there. My only regret was that it closed and then remained standing for some time afterwards empty.

I still go to where the Casino stood if I'm going up the motorway past Wigan and dream.

Tommy Cockburn
of Falkirk

In the last week of June 1974 a nineteen-year-old Scottish welder had an extra week's summer holiday to take. So, instead of moping around at home waiting for his mate to start his fortnight, he decided to go to Paignton in Devon a week early.

One night he went to Torquay and bumped into some guys from Stoke in a pub called the Yacht, got drinking and struck up a conversation with one in particular called Stephen (Dixie) Dean. A few hours later Dixie suggested that we go to the Compass Club just around the corner. OK, said the welder, who had no idea that his life was about to change for ever!

At this time I was a part-time DJ playing run of the mill pop and rock music (Quo, Roxy Music, etc.), and definitely not soul music. 'Come up to the top floor of the Compass,' says Dixie. 'You'll love it. They play real music up there.'

That music was Northern Soul, and the record playing was Junior Walker's 'I Ain't Going Nowhere'. My hair just stood on end. I just stood there thinking, 'I hate saxophone' and 'I don't like soul music', but my heart and feet definitely said otherwise. That whole holiday was spent at night in the Compass Club, watching people who loved this music flying across the dancefloor as if they had hovercrafts on their soles, spinning, clapping, back-dropping and having fun.

Just before he left, Dixie left me a box of singles, mostly Motown, and a few Emi discs. He gave them to me 1) because I had fallen in love with this thing called Northern Soul and 2) because he was getting married and wouldn't be needing them.

I went home with this box of goodies – all of which had a sticker on the label saying S Dean – and set about converting the locals to this amazing black dance music. My mate and I finally made it to Wigan Casino in March 1975. By then there were many people in Falkirk and the surrounding area who were converts.

After my first visit to the Casino, my love affair with the music and other devotees just grew and grew. Soon there were cars, more cars and buses coming down from Scotland to the all-nighters. Dozens and dozens of my friends and people that they knew got into the Northern scene, some fleetingly, many for the long haul, and some for reasons other than the music.

But one common thread ran true in all of them. They knew that they were with friends in that big dump of a dancehall in Wigan. Some of the people I got to know have remained friends for life. The one exception was my friend Hank, who sadly died of cancer a few years ago.

My memories of Wigan Casino are too numerous to mention. Where would you start? Hiring Russ and Richard to do my twenty-first at the Maniquis in Falkirk? Perhaps. Hearing the Velvet Satins for the first wonderful time? Possibly.

Everyone on the bus to Wigan having a whip-round so I could buy the original of the Velvet Satins (£30 in 1978), only to find it had a crack in it? Probably. The Beachcomber. A girl from London giving me a cuddle in the morning and saying thanks for making her feel good because all of us were having a great time? I think so.

Hearing 'Dust My Broom'? Yup. 'Three Before Eight'? Definitely. The people, the place, the atmosphere, the overwhelming friendliness? Most definitely. The tape recorders? Definitely.

Wigan Casino, the Northern Soul scene and all that went with it changed my life for ever and still affects it to this day. Whenever I DJ at a party locally there is always at least one person who wants to hear some Northern Soul and I still enjoy playing it. I wish it was the oldies all-nighter next Friday.

PS: There were two bad things about it all – the tea at the swimming pool always tasted hideous and the drive home!!!

Tommy Cockburn of Falkirk

1. 'Nothing Can Compare to You' Velvet Satins
2. 'Let's Go Somewhere' R Dean Taylor
3. 'Gotta Have Your Love' The Sapphires
4. 'The Next in Line' Hoagy Lands
5. 'I Gotta Let You Go' Martha and Vandellas
6. 'Better Use Your Head' Little Anthony and Imperials
7. 'Dust My Broom' Ike and Tina Turner
8. 'If You Ask Me' Jerry Williams
9. 'This Gets to Me' Pookie Hudson
10. 'The Three before Eight'

Steve Garner (Alf)
of Wigan

If anyone says to me the best days of their lives were their schooldays, then they didn't go to a Wigan Casino all-nighter. Since the Casino shut its doors for the last time, the golden days of soul music have been the topic of many conversations, over many a pint, and with many an old friend, both in Wigan and at various venues around the North-West.

My education into the Northern Soul scene started at Wigan Rugby Club, where Russ Winstanley was a DJ on Friday nights. When the Casino started their Friday night soul nights I followed (still not knowing what an all-nighter was). One of my first memories of that was Russ introducing a young lad with a leather jacket and long wispy hair who was DJ at the Va Va's in Bolton. He of course was Richard Searling and from then on the pair of them became *the* names on the Northern scene for the new breed of followers.

After meeting Russ through a mutual friend, I became a regular visitor to his newly opened record shop in Wigan and not long after I started visiting the all-nighters. The scene of 1,500 to 2,000 people chatting, buying and selling records and mainly dancing was unbelievable. I remember Russ getting a copy of a record called 'Manifesto'. It immediately became hugely popular and I was in the record booth upstairs in the Casino when the first copies went on sale.

I can only compare it to the present Argos catalogue advert on TV! We must have sold about 500 copies in half an hour! The big stars of US soul came to the Casino. The brilliant Junior Walker had me spellbound as I stood on the stage, not 20 feet away, watching this man play his sax, every note perfect.

The outstanding memory for me, and I'm sure a couple of thousand other people, was the night when an until recently unknown US soul singer came to Wigan. With one mid-70s track to go off, Betty Wright came to perform live. I got to the Casino later than usual that night and as I entered the main hall the electric atmosphere hit me. The place was absolutely packed, so hot that sweat was coming from the roof, and the set that Betty did was magical.

The atmosphere of the Casino had to be experienced to be believed. I have been to various nights since, but none have compared to the Casino.

The offshoots from the Casino were something not experienced by everybody, but all the same no less exciting. Russ and myself travelled to the Midlands for a gig only to find a social club in the middle of nowhere, no houses, just fields, and deserted except for the bar staff and manager. Within an hour the place was packed, everyone dancing to the latest Casino sounds.

Myself, Russ, Richard and Doreen used to play football and tennis in the street outside Russ's shop while the latest batch of hits were winging their way to us from the States.

However, the last memory must be the one that everyone who went to the Casino experienced. Ten past eight on a Sunday morning, outside the Casino coming down from the high of the previous night, saying goodbye to friends old and new and waiting for 12 o'clock the following Saturday.

That went on for years for many thousands of people. But in the end, 'Time Will Pass You By'.

Steve Garner (Alf) of Wigan

1. 'Determination' Dean Parrish
2. 'You Didn't Say a Word' Yvonne Baker
3. 'Stick by Me, Baby' Salvadors
4. 'I'm Gonna Change' Four Seasons
5. 'It Really Hurts Me, Girl' Carstairs

6. 'Hung Up on Your Love' Montclairs
7. 'Don't It Make You Feel Funky?' Joe Hicks
8. 'I'm Coming Home in the Morning' Lou Pride
9. 'Keep on Talkin' ' James Barnett
10. 'Time Will Pass You By' Tobi Legend

Dave Shaw
of Nuneaton (formerly of Wolverhampton)

It is 4am on Sunday morning, 26 September 1975. The four of us who made the journey from Wolverhampton last night are standing outside a large decrepit dancehall called Wigan Casino.

This is Wigan, an old-fashioned town in the heart of the industrial North. Famous for its Rugby League team and for the Heart of Soul music in the UK, Wigan Casino.

I had dreamt of this night for a full year, and now here I was outside the most famous disco in the world. I was ten weeks short of my fifteenth birthday. What do I remember about the first night? I remember that it was the second anniversary and the first record I danced to in Wigan was 'My Sugar Baby' by Connie Clark.

I can remember Tommy Hunt coming on stage and the manager, Mike Walker, making an emotional speech. Most of all I remember being on the balcony, watching almost 2,000 people dance, and the incredible warmth and friendship emanating from those people. The lasting impression I got from that wonderful night was a feeling of coming home, finding where I belonged and where I wanted to be. I knew that even at fourteen years old I would never give up the Northern Soul scene.

Wigan Casino closed its doors for the last time in 1981 and I was there that night too. I didn't stay until the very end. I left around 8.30am. To me the death of the Casino became like some kind of circus and I didn't want to witness the last rites. The last record I danced to in Wigan was Dutch Robinson's 'Can't Get Along without You'. After that I walked out without a backward glance. I cried all the way home.

Wigan may have been the biggest part of my twenty years on the scene, but it was only a part. When the Casino closed we had Peterborough and Rotherham, and then Stafford's Top of the World. Today there is still a hard core of people like me who just can't get enough.

I have to mention the friends who did not make it: Ruth from Worcester, Roch from Yate, Mike Rolo from Wigan, Penny (Fish) Fisher from Kidderminster, Martin Randall from Kingswinford and, from Wolverhampton, Steve (Mozza) Morris, Bryn Lane and Phil Shelton. God bless them all.

Lots of memories, lots of laughs and a few tears. But now, more than twenty years on, my love for the music is still as strong as it was on that freezing night in Wigan back in 1975.

Paul Donnelly
from Peterborough

Wigan Casino was many things to many different folk. To some it was the records, to some it was the atmosphere, to some it was the crack. To some it was everything in life.

I had a two-year relationship with the Casino, starting in September 1973 and finishing in early 1976. It is difficult now, looking back, to remember why I stopped going. For sure, the type of music being offered at the time was not to my liking, although it seemed to be entertaining the paying punters who packed the dancefloor. If 1,000 dancers want to dance to 'Hawaii 5-0' then fine, brilliant, but not for me.

However, the Casino for those two years when I attended was fantastic and, though I enjoyed smaller clubs more like the Torch, it had a unique atmosphere.

Although it was not as intense as the smaller clubs, it was on some nights fully charged and very electric. 1972–3 was my era and the quality of music introduced during this period was fantastic. It was my music and no one could take it away.

What did the Casino mean to me? Well, at the time, nothing. It was a venue that we supported and we enjoyed it, but then in 1992 I was asked by Steve Thompson to DJ at an oldies night at Hindley near Wigan.

I arrived early and decied to visit where the Casino stood. I parked my car, walked up the cobblestone road and rested my arms on some railings and looked over at some flat offices. I don't mind admitting I filled up, lump in the throat, I became very upset. Why? Because Wigan Casino *did* matter. It was the greatest underground music venue the world will ever see. And I was part of it!

Looking back, those train journeys from Peterborough to Wigan were unbelievable. Peterborough change at Leicester, Leicester change at Birmingham, Birmingham change at Crewe, then Wigan.

The journey back on a Sunday morning would normally take seven hours, although someone I know did not get back until 11.30am on Monday, after getting on the wrong train and ending up in Glasgow.

The following from Peterborough to Wigan during 1973–6 was large and it was quite a sight on Peterborough station at 6.30pm, waiting for Don Thomas ('Come on, Train'). I know I speak for the hundreds of people from our area who supported the Casino when I say thank you for some wonderful weekends.

On a final note, anybody who reads this book, who never had the privilege of actually attending the Casino, will read, digest, ponder and believe they understand what it was all about. *No Way!*

Paul Donnelly of Peterborough

1. 'You Didn't Say a Word' Yvonne Baker
2. 'Now You've Got the Upper Hand' Candi Staton
3. 'I've Got to Find Me Somebody' The Vel-Vets
4. 'I Can't Help Lovin' You' Paul Anka
5. 'Tell Me Why' Life
6. 'What Can I Do?' Billy Prophet
7. 'You Don't Love Me Any More' Johnny Caswell
8. 'Double Cookin' ' Checkerboard Squares
9. 'She's Putting You On' United Four
10. 'Stronger Than Her Love' The Flirtations

Dave Ward
of Leyland, near Preston

It was well after midnight on a freezing December Saturday night in 1977 and finally I was in!

I had wriggled, shoved and forced my way through the crush of people at the door, charmed my passage through the grim-faced, tuxedoed bouncers guarding the stairwell and survived the icy scrutiny of the cashdesk lady, who checked my green Casino membership card as thoroughly as a Soviet border guard, as well as relieving my wallet of two quid.

As I climbed the steep flights of stairs, I hitched the black all-night bag on to my right shoulder, hooking my thumb through the strap in true Northern Soul fashion. I was on my own, as usual, although as a Casino regular I was on 'nodding terms' with some of the 'faces' who made up the Northern scene.

The faces who mattered at the Casino were split into three main groups. First, the Soul Experts, the record collectors and dealers who swapped handfuls of fivers in the downstairs bar, buying and selling the rare soul records from Detroit and Chicago that were the lifeblood of the Northern Soul scene in the mid-70s. Then the Soul Boys, ultra-cool poseurs who wore expensive calf-length leather coats, tailor-made jackets, trousers in the latest multi-pocket, 30in parallel style, the best-looking girls on their arms and hand-stitched Nottingham brogues on their feet. And finally the Dancefloor Aces, an élitist faction that put the buzz into Northern Soul. Dancers dictated the DJs' play-lists, made or broke new soul records and generally set the pace and style of the soul music played at any club. The pace they set at the Casino all-nighters was faster, more frantic and hard-driving than in any other soul club.

I pushed open the double doors into the main hall of the Casino, feeling the adrenalin building up into a stomach-churning, heart-pounding excitement as the heat and sweat of an all-night soul club, already packed with over 1,000 people, hit me like a blow from a hot, damp, Brut-soaked towel. The noise was incredible! Huge banks of loudspeakers ranging the stage front powered the throbbing bass and drum beats across the dancefloor like a sonic wave, while soaring strings and screaming saxophones seared overhead, making my eardrums 'pop' and my fist tighten around the strap of my nighter bag.

Weaving my way down the left-hand side of the dancefloor was like walking the length of a football pitch. The Casino's dancefloor was huge, bordered on three sides by a forest of pillars supporting the high balcony, creating a dark shadowy world beneath them, holding nests of tables and chairs in cavern-like alcoves. I reached the alcove under the stairs and made my first stop, slinging my bag on to a table, and changed into clothes suitable for a would-be Dancefloor Ace: short-sleeved black sweatshirt, black pleat front parallel 28s, thin white cotton socks and black spit-shined, soft-soled leather shoes. I changed quickly, tightened the thin leather belt around my waist, packed my street clothes and shoes into the bag, shouldered it and made my way to the stage front. A last stop at one of the mirrored pillars to check that my appearance, from the cropped hair to the tips of my polished shoes, was in order, and I stepped out on to the floor.

I passed through the left-hand corner and threw my bag up on to the centre speaker cabinet so that I could see it from the dancefloor. Sitting on the edge of the stage, I jammed half a stick of gum into my mouth and watched the guys in the right-hand corner back-dropping and spinning as they danced to the Drifters' classic 'You've Got to Pay Your Dues'. Yeah ... they were good, but I considered the old stomp and acrobatics of the Northern 'Stompers' rather clumsy. Russ Winstanley intro-duced the next record, Art Freeman's 'Slippin' Around', and my eyes swivelled over to the right as I watched the élite of the left-hand corner warming up, directly beneath the bank of speakers, under the brightest ultraviolet light, surrounded by onlookers and packed with the fastest and most modern dancers at the Casino. It was a hot spot, the hardest-worked section of dancefloor in the world, and to me a Northern Soul paradise!

The left-hand corner was not for me. I'd danced a little left from centre two weeks ago: an elbow in the ribs, an 'accidental' stomp on the foot and a derisive sneer had convinced me that I wasn't yet up to the required standard – good enough for the front, but not that good! Still, I had been spared the worst, a large gap opening around the unfortunate dancer who found his every step being mimicked by a dozen or so souls until he fled in embarrassment, back to the anonymity of the middle of the tightly packed floor. Only at the front was there room to really dance, and places at the front were hard-earned ... Still, one advantage of being at the Casino alone was that I had nothing else to do except dance all night!

The DJ was playing the awful dirge by Al Kent, 'The Way You've Been Acting Lately', so I took the chance of sliding off to the upstairs bar for a Coke, pushing through the crowds of soul fans to get along the balcony to the bar, hoping to get back to the stage before the next record started. Russ was playing Phillip Mitchell's 'Free for All' by the time I returned, so, leaning against the stage, I watched the seething floor. On my left, the stomp and back-drop specialists, spinning like ice-skaters. In the centre the controlled float of the 'Cool Offs' sliding at double time in a sweat-free, Highland Room-style zone. Over on my right the regional mix of the left-hand corner, guys from Newcastle, Manchester, Dudley, Lancaster, Preston and London, were half dancing, half messing around, giving the record the sort of contemptible attention reserved for the best dancers as they wait for something better.

I'd been on the floor for nearly an hour. Sweat ran down my face in rivulets and my shirt was soaked through. I bopped about a bit to Major Lance's 'Investigate', gave the floor some hammer to Phil Loman's 'Rock Me' and was starting to get serious when the DJ played himself out with the stomper standard 'I worship You, Baby' by the Glories. I swung up to sit on the stage as the girl on my right gave the Casino hand signal for 'Lend me a swig of your Coke ...' so I passed the bottle across and watched my Coke go from mouth to mouth along the entire stage front, never to be seen again, as Richard Searling took over the mike. 'Thanks to Russ for the last ninety minutes ... Here's Otis Blackwell and 'It's All Over Me!'

It was a sound with all the essential ingredients for a dancefloor maniac: fast, tricky and with a filthy beat ... I dropped to the floor at the same time as the entire left-hand corner ... spun around ... picked up the double-beat and found myself in the middle of hell!!!

I knew I was in deep trouble. Flashing feet rocked and bounced around me. I was forced over into the corner, found some space and made it mine, face to face with Charlie from Lancaster, one of the best dancers I'd ever seen, but I was flying ... I blew out the dancer behind me, created more space and hit the double-beat as I spun on to my left leg ... I was really feeling good ... My shadow, highlighted by the overhead UV light was smooth and fluid on the shiny maple dancefloor, allowing me to get a mirror image of my style as I began to get 'out of myself'.

I'd heard other dancers talk about 'losing themselves' but now I knew what they meant ... I was gone – fluid, fast, double-beat – I felt great!!! Then Charlie was in my face ... He winked and a second later lifted his arms up from the elbow and blew me away!!! Left-hand corner brilliance against grim determination.

The record ended and I crashed out on to the stage, gasping for breath, turning around when a Coke bottle was sloshed in front of my face. I gulped some down and passed the bottle along to the next guy along. 'Thanks, mate,' said Charlie, draining the bottle. 'You wanna move your bag over here ... Somebody'll nick it!'

From that moment on, I never danced anywhere else but in the left-hand corner when at Wigan Casino. That piece of dancefloor was the best dance surface I ever found at an all-nighter. The nights I spent there were quite simply the best nights out I ever had.

Dave Ward of Leyland

1. 'Ain't Nothing You Can Do' Joe Matthews
2. 'It's All Over Me' Otis Blackwell
3. 'Talking 'Bout Poor Folks' Lou Edwards and Today's People
4. 'The Champion' Willie Mitchell
5. 'Love You, Baby' Eddie Parker
6. 'There was a Time' Gene Chandler
7. 'Time' Edwin Starr
8. 'Lend a Hand' Bobby Hutton
9. 'My Hang-up is You' Skullsnaps
10. 'I Can See Him Loving You' Anderson Brothers

Dave Ward's Radical 'Left-hand Corner' Sounds

1. 'Do What You Feel' Rimshots
2. 'The Trip' Dave Mitchell and the Screamers

3. 'So is the Sun' World Column
4. 'Summer in the Parks' East Coast Connection
5. 'Crazy Changes' Luv
6. 'Who Says Honkies ain't Got Soul?' Bang Gang
7. 'Cat's Eyes' Life
8. 'Find My Way' Cameo
9. 'Captain of My Ship' Seventh Wonder
10. 'Biyo' Earth Wind and Fire

The Casino may be dead and gone, but part of it lives on … in the kitchen of a house in Wigan!

Andrew and Fiona Nevin were both fanatical Casino-goers and joined the legions of souvenir hunters when the building was finally closed. But they went one better than those who nicked the odd poster and piece of carpet by buying some of the famous maplewood dancefloor.

Andrew then put it down in his kitchen, and even though the couple have now emigrated to Australia, the wood which was trodden on by so many thousands of pairs of feet has remained behind in pristine condition.

Hairdresser Andrew was working in a salon near to the Casino when it was being demolished. He got chatting to the demolition men and asked how much they wanted for the dancefloor.

'I eventually got it for £90. I was also going to buy the grand piano that was on the stage, but I didn't have the room,' he said.

By the way, folks, who remembers the night the curtains opened on stage to reveal a certain DJ in a compromising position with a young lady behind that same piano? The breathless romeo covered his embarrassment and bowed and waved to everyone on the dancefloor!

Anyway Andrew and Fiona moved to Avoca Beach, New South Wales, eight years ago and found that the long reach of Northern Soul and the Casino had even touched Down Under.

According to Andrew:

We have been in Australia for just over eight years and about the only thing we miss are the soul scene and the lunatics who spent the weekend travelling and dancing all night in a sweaty run-down club that did not sell alcohol.

How do you explain that to the average Pom, never mind an Aussie? But never fear, we had been in Australia for about three years when I was reading a music magazine and saw an advertisement for a Northern Soul night in Sydney. The club is situated in the red light area of King's Cross. Being the intrepid travellers we are, we parked the car and walked up Oxford Street towards the cross, dodging the transvestites, prostitutes and drunks. As we got closer to the club we knew this was going to be our kind of night out.

It was run by a Sydney DJ, George, who calls himself Agent Double O Soul. He got into Northern Soul by reading about it in *Blues and Soul* and record-collecting magazines. He has a large collection of good records and a crowd of skinheads and scooter boys attend the nights.

George has also organized some all-nighters, which are pretty well attended. A crowd came up from Melbourne, twelve hours' driving non-stop, and from Brisbane, which is about the same distance. One guy from Melbourne, Vince Peach, used to go to the Twisted Wheel and is a mad record collector. Vince does a local radio show and plays Northern sounds. He is running an all-nighter in Melbourne, so, as you can see, we still get a dose of soul music, although not often enough.

What do I remember about the Casino? Well, I met Fiona there and we are still together twenty years later. Fiona was fanatical about dancing and fast sounds.

We used to spend a lot of time there, Monday, Wednesday

and Friday early sessions, and at one time you could go to Gerrys Inn on Tuesdays and Thursdays. Then there were the Friday and Saturday all-nighters. Our best memories are the oldies in Mr M's when it was really packed, then going down to the baths in the morning and being searched by the drug squad. In the early days getting past Mrs Woods on the door was part of the fun.

We even had our own terminology: divvies were people who went to pubs and got drunk and went to discos; gear was, well, you know what it was; and the squad was the drug squad.

We had a great time at the Casino. It was very memorable and I am so glad I was part of it. I met friends from all over the country and travelled to all-nighters all over England and Scotland.

Andrew and Fiona Nevin of Avoca Beach, NSW, Australia (Formerly of Wigan)

1. 'The Who Who Song' Jackie Wilson
2. 'The Snake' Al Wilson
3. 'Dust My Broom' Ike and Tina Turner
4 'Have Some Everybody' Flaming Emeralds
5. 'Sliced Tomatoes' Just Brothers
6. 'These Boots Were Made for Walking' Happy Cats
7. 'Ain't Nothing but a Houseparty' Showstoppers
8. 'Love Factory' Eloise Laws
9. 'Get It Off My Conscience' Lovelites
10. 'It's All Over' Charles Mann

Ian Palmer, who with his friend Dennis Lee runs the Northern Soul fanzine *Manifesto*, has good and bad memories of the Casino.

The good times involve the music, the friendliness and the atmosphere of the great venue. The bad times involve being freezing cold trying to hitch a lift from a village near Gloucester to the all-nighters.

Ian was a teenager with no car in those days, and together with friends like DJ Dave Thorley would regularly scrape together enough money for a trip North.

'It was a horrible trip, to get up there without any transport. Most of my memories of going to Wigan are of standing around on service stations with a box of records, trying to thumb a lift,' recalled Ian.

His passion for soul was fired in the mid-1970s through youth clubs and characters in the Midlands like John 'Kojak' Harvey. Bald-headed John looked like the famous American TV detective and he spent his shows sitting on the front of the stage handing out lollipops, while a sidekick played the records.

'It sounds really naff now, but he was a real showman and everyone had a good laugh,' said Ian.

The lure of the Casino proved too great and by 1975 Ian was attending as often as money would allow. In between there were all-nighters at Yate, Redditch and elsewhere to cater for the nationwide demand for Northern Soul events.

Said Ian: 'The Casino was *the* place to hear the sounds that were coming out, not the stuff that everyone else was playing. There was no such thing as an oldies scene then, really, it was all excellent new records and some favourites.

'The Casino had incredibly good points and a few bad points. I was never really into the slightly naff image of badges, baggy pants and Keep the Faith stuff. But otherwise the friendship and the music were brilliant. You could hear anything there. And everyone was equal, there was nothing élitist about it.'

Casino manager **Mike Walker,** who sadly died in 1980, recalled in a special article written for the sixth anniversary of the Casino all-nighters how he had become involved with the most successful club in Britain.

I remember the first time I set foot in Wigan I'd been temporarily transferred to help out with the advance booking for the Beatles show at the town's ABC Cinema. I'd been working a few miles down the road at their cinema in Leigh and, at sixteen, the prospect of being involved with a live show as opposed to films was about one of the most exciting things that had happened in my short working career.

I had only just moved to Lancashire the previous year, having lived in a number of towns up and down the country, finishing my schooling in Carlisle, the town in which I was born fifteen years before.

Ever since I can remember, my father has worked in the entertainment business, working in theatres and cinemas, so it didn't really come as much of a surprise that I should follow in his footsteps in my first job. To be exact I did try my hand for a few months after leaving school working in beat groups, but £8 a night between four even in those days wasn't much to live on.

I did in fact stay at the Wigan ABC for four years as assistant manager, and for the first eighteen months almost every fortnight a live package tour worked a one-nighter at our theatre. The Rolling Stones, Hollies, Tom Jones, Roy Orbison, all packed the hall during that time, and I still can't get over the night that Marvin Gaye, Diana Ross, the Supremes, Stevie Wonder and several other of Motown's stars all appeared together on one bill and played to a half-empty house – of course, that was 1964.

I made many friends in Wigan during that time and was very sad when I was transferred to Manchester (only for a short time, I'm glad to say, as it happened). During my stay in Manchester I became a member at the Twisted Wheel. Their Saturday all-nighters were something else, the atmosphere was dynamite.

Some of the acts that worked there are now considered legends. Can you imagine the night Otis Redding appeared? Enough said! After six months I returned to work in Wigan – although things had changed. The live package shows were becoming less frequent and somehow the atmosphere wasn't the same around the place. I think the prospect of becoming a cinema manager was not as exciting as I had imagined, and everyone else seemed to be having a good time at night while I was having to work. So at nineteen I decided to spread my wings and look around for another job.

One of my friends was working for a local newspaper and when a vacancy occurred, he suggested that I apply. I got the job and remained there for several happy years.

Gerry Marshall was then the manager at the Casino and while attending a function one evening at the club we started chatting and he offered me a job as the DJ in the Beachcomber, the Casino's under-eighteens room. I must admit I was somewhat flattered by his offer and felt that the opportunity was not to be missed, so, with many reservations about my own capability, I decided to accept.

Within six months I was working for Gerry five nights per week, progressing into the main hall at the Casino, and must admit I was enjoying my new career as Wigan's newest spinner. Gerry and I became very close friends during this time and when he told me that he was considering buying the business, I was once again flattered at his offer to me to be manager of the club.

Russ Winstanley was also DJing in Wigan at the same time as myself and was building quite a name for himself with his soul nights at the Rugby Club and the Newtown British Legion – we did in fact get to know each other through my buying my soul imports from his record stall – and when I became manager I approached Russ regarding him running a soul stall within the club itself.

During these early days our regulars were being lost to the Torch all-nighter in Stoke and, although we were playing the big sounds, we could not emulate the incredible atmosphere the Torch had with its all-nighter.

Russ suggested that we try a one-off at the Casino at approximately the same time as the Torch's lease was due for renewal and with Gerry's blessing, on 23 September 1973, the Wigan Casino all-nighter was born. The story has been told many times over about the incredible success the Casino all-nighters have become, and with six years' history the place has become a legend in its own time.

Russ and I still talk about 1973 as if it was only yesterday. It is just amazing how the whole time has passed. Like most things, many of the people have changed with the times, our individual roles altering. I myself am presently very heavily involved with RK Records, and also many outside promotions. Russ and Richard likewise are both employed in the record business.

Gerry has also developed his business interests, and many of the DJs and staff have left the Casino for good and gone on to even greater things, but without a doubt everyone – including myself – who has passed through those two famous black doors in Station Road has got an awful lot to thank Wigan Casino for. Long may it live.

David Ball of Soft Cell told *The Face*:

I started going to Northern Soul clubs in Blackpool, where I lived, in the spring of 1975, when I was fifteen or sixteen ... the two main ones were the Blackpool Casino (part of the Pleasure Beach Complex) and the Highland Room at the Blackpool Mecca. Sometimes I'd go up to Wigan but usually I couldn't take the pace because I was working every day as an ice-cream man on Blackpool beach.

Northern Soul was the first music I ever danced to or took seriously. It was an alternative to Gary Glitter for kids like me. Of course, the dancing at Wigan was intimidating – the first time I went I just stood in a corner with my mouth open, but no one noticed. Blackpool – especially the Mecca – was less scary, perhaps just because I knew more people. Anyway, all the clubs I went to were very friendly places; I never saw one fight.

People went along just because they loved the music and wanted to dance to records like 'Queen of Fools' by Barbara Mills and 'The Afternoon of the Rhino' by the Mike Post Coalition. Illegal bootlegs and acetates sold for a bomb and rare record collecting was very competitive ... the most I ever paid was £7 for the original of 'Skiing in the Snow', a prized possession!

We often used chalk dust or talcum powder to make spinning and sliding easier and for dancing I always wore flat shoes, white socks (very important!) and Birmingham Bags – straight baggy trousers in canvas or cord with a high waistband and lots of buttons ... the obsession with detail was quite surprising.

Then we'd all have the same black macs and when you went on an all-nighter you always took your change of clothes in a holdall, preferably covered with badges from different clubs to show how dedicated you were. I had the original all-nighter badge from Wigan Casino and their Night Owl one too.

I still play the music at home and scour junk shops and markets for Northern Soul bargains! And, of course, it was all a very strong influence on what I'm doing now ... and I don't just mean recording 'Tainted Love'. There was a rawness in those records, a rough edge and imperfection that I loved and that's directly affected how we do things in Soft Cell; leaving in the odd mistake, not overdubbing too much and so on.

What's more important, I think, is the overall impression a record leaves and those old soul songs evoke a really magical nostalgia in me. They were good times ...

Steve Strange told *The Face*:

I started getting into the Northern Soul scene when I was fourteen through my cousin; we'd go up North, a whole crowd of us from Wales, for the weekend. It wasn't just for the Wigan Casino Saturday nights, though, we did a whole weekend, non-stop. We'd go to Samantha's in Sheffield on Friday night, then straight on to an all-dayer at Blackpool Mecca on Saturday, then to Wigan on Saturday night; then on Sunday afternoons there was a revival of the Torch club in Manchester. You didn't need anyone to put you up, you just kept going the whole time.

When I first went up there I was just amazed at the dancing – back-flips, somersaults and acrobatics ... and the atmosphere. Wigan Casino was the friendliest club I've ever known. We were just like brothers and sisters.

It was like a religion to those people, and if you were part of it, you just had to be at all those all-nighters. No one cared about clothes or posing: we just wore baggy trousers, cricket shirts or vests and flat brogues with leather soles that slid easily.

The music was great, although there was a split between the rarer import soul scene played at Wigan and the New Northern Soul brought in by the Blackpool Mecca DJ Ian Levine, which was more funky and commercial and meant a slightly different dancing style. I remember my girlfriend winning a dancing competition at Wigan and it not going down too well because she danced the new Northern Soul way.

Some kids would pay up to £100 for a rare soul record – they'd just have the one. I used to have a few collectors' pieces but I never paid that much for them. In fact I found one of the most valuable – *Major Lance Live at the Torch* – in a junk shop, which was incredible. I still listen to that music, like my favourites Gloria Jones's 'Tainted Love', Keenya Collins's 'Love Bandit' or the Ric Tic Relics compilation.

I suppose I left all that behind because I wanted to get out of Wales and into something different, but Northern Soul will continue ... always.

Tony Gordon of Blue Rondo told *The Face*:

I grew up in Bournemouth but luckily for me some lads from up North opened a couple of Northern Soul clubs in town called Busters and Pandoras. This is about 1973–4, when I was sixteen – I heard the music, saw the dancing, got completely hooked and started travelling up to the Wigan Casino, a Cleethorpes club (we called it the East Coast Connection!) and the Blackpool Mecca all-dayers.

The first Northern club I ever went to was in Manchester on a Saturday night and afterwards we all went to the football stadium and got a coach to Wigan. We'd dance all night there and then continue next door at the Beachcomber, which opened at 7am. Not that it was all happening up North though ... there were all-nighters at St Ives in Huntingdon and the last one I went to was at Yate near Bristol.

Northern Soul was a scene that revolved around records, dancing and gear. It was the ultimate escapism – as I believe music still is – and it provided an alternative to fighting and excessive alcohol consumption ... both of which I'd been into before. No one actually taught you how to dance up there, you just watched and learned ... although I do think the gymnastics element was a bit much at times. All those Russian rolls and back-flips: sometimes it just wasn't dancing but at least it kept you fit!

As for the music, I still love it and listen to it: records like the Ivorys' 'Please Stay', Linda Jones's 'I Just Can't Live My Life' and Spyder Turner's 'I Can't Make It Any More'. Personally, I don't use the term 'Northern Soul' ... it's just great American soul music.

That music's been an obvious influence on what Blue Rondo are doing ... particularly since our guitarist Mark Riley did the all-nighters too.

But it wasn't just about clubs and music in those days; like any scene it relied on the people involved ... and they were great! They looked just like anyone else, but what a bunch of extreme personalities. Mind games were very much a part of the all-nighter scene – playing tricks, having fun with people – and kids would turn up with false noses and ears or go round talking in rhyme. I remember one guy set up a Wendy house outside Wigan Casino and sat there with a hankie on his head waving to everyone. They were mad!

I think the magic of that scene was lost for me around 1979, when the drugs thing got really out of hand: there were constant raids by the drug squad and many sick incidents, like when some pretty stupid people sold amphetamine sulphate cut with rat poison and there were a lot of very ill kids around. Luckily I missed out on that, but one thing that whole era taught me was that it's not smart to take drugs.

Former Wigan Casino DJ **Kev Roberts** is now a partner in Goldmine Soul Supply, prolific producers of CDs aimed at the Northern Soul market.

The company has more than seventy titles on its books, using master tapes from the vaults of record companies which own previously super-rare recordings.

Goldmine has enjoyed particular success with its compilations *The Wigan Casino Story*, Parts One and Two, *The Blackpool Mecca Story*, *The Torch Story*, and *The Twisted Wheel Story*.

Kev also has his own radio show on Magic 828, serving Leeds and West Yorkshire. In an article he wrote for the Northern Soul magazine *Manifesto*, he explained his involvement with the Casino, how he discovered a Top Twenty hit – 'The Flasher' by Lloyd Michels – and possibly lost a fortune.

By the age of sixteen Kev had begun DJing at soul clubs and attending all-nighters at the Torch, Va Va's in Bolton and Blackpool Mecca. One night he found himself at the second-ever Casino all-nighter, on 30 September 1973.

'As I walked in I thought, "Crikey, this is a big place." It looked like there were about 600 in that night and the place held 2,500. They were playing an awful lot of pressings, stuff out on Jay Boy, etc. and I thought, "This is crap, the Mecca has got the best rarities," which to be fair it did at the time.'

His friends from Nottingham pushed him to the front and he was introduced to Russ Winstanley. Kev takes up the story:

Russ said: 'Who are you?' I said: 'Kev Roberts, and I'm from Nottingham.' Anyway he put me on and thanks to the helpful enthusiasm of my crowd from the East Midlands I went down well. I must have made the right impression, because Russ said: 'Do you want to work here every week?' So I said: 'Yeah.'

My fee in those days was £10 a night and the DJ line-up was Russ, Ian Fishwick and myself, and the three of us did the whole night. The following week we had about 1,000 in, and the week after that even more. Suddenly the pressure was on, my name was known and I was expected to keep getting the new records.

I was hungry and started finding my own sounds with the help of Simon Soussan. By late October Ian Fishwick was being frozen out of the situation, mainly because he didn't have the tunes.

Russ had some songs, but I probably had the best ones, because of my connections. Russ was on the look-out for another DJ and I remember saying there's a guy called Richard S, who had some great stuff at Va Va's in Bolton. The next thing I knew, Richard had joined us. Suddenly we had a new credibility and this new easy to get to venue. By December 1973 we were rocketing, with attendances up to around 1,500 or 1,600.

So to 1974 and the buzz word was Northern Soul. I was only seventeen years old and we were breaking new ground with a sound of our own. Songs like Lou Ragland's 'I Travel Alone', and some more commercial stuff like 'The Joker' and 'Strings a Go Go'.

Now the commercial angle started to appear. With regular attendances of over 2,000, music industry people started to appear. *Blues and Soul* were up there practically every week. Television cameras started appearing for the first time and Northern Soul was a household name.

Eventually the outside commercial pressures forcing us to play more and more records like 'Footsee' that were guaranteed floor-packers led to my departure from the Casino.

So in 1975 I went back to my real love – record collecting. I don't feel bitter about it. When something becomes as successful as the Casino did, such forces are bound to come into play. But I must admit, after leaving the Casino I did feel left out in the cold for a bit, seeing the enormous success that it continued to have for the rest of the 70s.

After the Casino I decided to go to New York to see what I could find. While there I met Lloyd Michels, who had this demo disc of a track called 'The Flasher', which I brought back to England to get a record deal with. First I tried 20th Century Records, who had released 'Reaching for the Best' (The Exciters). They didn't want to know, and so I went off to a reggae label called Creole in London, who also didn't like it. They put me in touch with Dennis Berger, who was the label manager for Route, who picked it up, and it became a big hit.

It was even used as the theme tune on Radio 1's *Newsbeat*, but I didn't make any money out of it because I was young and naive. It was even featured on *Top of the Pops*. I was invited down to London to watch the recording, but I couldn't afford the train fare and I was too busy talking Northern. I just wanted to find records.

During the late 70s I met up with a record-buying customer of mine called Les McCutcheon from Weybridge in Surrey who was a businessman, a little older than me and he knew what was what. He became my partner, importing records and making things for Casino Classics like 'I'm Going to Share It with You' by Diana Foster and things like 'Green Onions' by Mod 79. When *Quadrophenia* came out, we were dabbling in all sorts of things.

Then an outfit who were making records for us called the Nicky North Band had a stab at a jazz funk record called 'Steppin' '. We pressed up 1,000 white labels and sold them to a store called the Record Shack, who then reordered it, by which time we needed a name ... Record Shack ... Shakatak, and they went on to be signed by Polydor.

I remember Les saying to me as clear as day: 'Are you in or are you out?' And as we had only gotten a £500 advance between the lot of us I thought there was more money in trying to find another 'Better Use Your Head' by Little Anthony and the Imperials than there was in this jazz funk game, so short-sightedly I let it go, and Kev Roberts lost another fortune.

Former Wigan Casino oldies DJ **Brian Rae**

The Casino came along at the right time and was *the* thing in the 70s. It gave a lot of people a lot of enjoyment. If you look at the other venues of the time, like Cleethorpes, although they were successful they didn't have the same drawing power as the Casino.

Brian was one of the few DJs to work the club before the all-nighters were even created. The veteran soul DJ, who also spun the sounds at the famous Twisted Wheel in Manchester, found himself hired to do a 'normal' show at the Casino on a Monday night in the early 1970s.

At that time he had two girl dancers working with him, and during a break when Mike Walker took over the decks, Brian rushed off to get changed into drag. The place was full and Brian nervously waited for his hilarious entrance back on to the stage wearing a swimsuit beneath a dress to join the girl dancers.

He bounded on ... and found the place almost empty. 'There were only about ten people left in. Apparently they had all gone for the last bus,' Brian recalls drily.

On to more serious things, he was asked by Russ Winstanley to join the line-up of DJs about a year after the all-nighters were launched. At that time Brian had DJed at the Up the Junction in Crewe and other venues around the Wigan area. He well remembers many months earlier a conversation with Alan Day and Tony Jebb in Warrington, when they invited him to go with them to the Casino:

It was about three months into the Casino starting up and they said they were going up there. They said it would have been worth me going along, but the place would be shut down pretty soon anyway so there was no point. Then they drove off in Alan's sports car and that was that.

Of course, they were wrong and the Casino went on for eight years. I never minded the commercialization, because my belief is that the more people that like soul music the better. It's there for enjoyment, not to be a close-knit community, although that does happen.

Even today Keele is good because it's a social event. They don't even need to advertise because everyone knows when the next one is on. That was just how the oldies all-nighters at the Casino used to be.

It's great that so many people have grown up, got divorced or whatever, and are now back on the scene. It's almost like a big singles club!

Former Casino DJ **Pat Brady**

The Casino shaped my life. It has influenced me ever since. I was saying to a youngster the other day that Wigan was the rave scene of the 1970s. It's very, very similar in many ways to the current dance scene. The dance scene encompasses the good, the bad and ugly of what Wigan was about.

Former Casino DJ **Steve Whittle**

Being a Wigan lad I went to the Casino to the soul nights before they started having all-nighters. Some of the Friday nights they did even then had some great acts on. I saw the Tams, Edwin Starr, Jimmy Ruffin and others. You could see the potential of the building, but nobody realized that the all-nighters would go on for that long.

The soul scene had graduated from fairly small clubs to this massive venue. Va Va's in Bolton, which was the first one I went to, was only about the same size as the Beachcomber at the Casino, which we used to use as a warm-up venue to get people off the streets before the all-nighter started!

When you think that the Casino ran an all-nighter every week, plus the oldies every month, for eight years, it was incredible. I don't think there's any venue now that could get crowds as good as that. Some all-nighters now which are on about four times a year would be delighted to get in the numbers that Wigan did every single week.

Ady Croasdell
of Kent Records and the 100 Club All-nighters

I first started going to Wigan in the early days before the boom. I enjoyed the place. I remember the oldies all-nighters best because I went to them religiously. I knew all my friends were going to be there. I was a record dealer by then and we were still getting bargains, making discoveries and bringing stuff back from the States and it was great fun.

I used to go to Wigan dressed as a punk and I never got any trouble from anyone. The Casino had a great atmosphere. One of the silliest things was when me and my mate Mick Smith found a copy of a Tony Blackburn LP with 'I'll Do Anything' (the Doris Troy song) on it. I gave it to Keith Minshull to play as Lenny Gamble and he did. It was just supposed to be a joke. When he played it and everyone danced to it I thought that maybe the punters weren't too discerning.

Little Scotty
of Wolverhampton, promoter of the Blackburn All-nighters

I got into soul when I was sixteen. I used to go to places like the Catacombs in Wolverhampton and youth clubs and places like that. One day I met a lad from Rochdale who told me that an all-nighter had started in Wigan.

That was it – I started going in 1974 and I went for six years. Once Wigan started getting in the press and they were talking about drugs, my dad wanted to stop me going. So I had a rest for six months and started going again. I used to catch the coach from Wolverhampton run by a lad called Jethro. He was a good dancer and the kids would watch him and go away and practise and then next week they would all be dancing like him! There were a lot of good dancers and spinners from Wolverhampton.

Wigan will go down in history, just like the Torch and the Wheel, and probably Keele when that eventually closes. I have still got magazines and memorabilia and all kinds of things from when it started, and up on the wall I've got a big glossy picture of the front of the Casino with all the crowd outside.

Current Favourite Sounds at the Blackburn All-nighters, Tony's Express Ballroom (June 1996)

1. 'Winner Take All' Geraldine Hunt
2. 'Follow Your Heart' Bunny Sigler
3. 'Never for Me' Millionaires
4. 'Working on Your Case' O'Jays
5. 'Say It's Something' Billy Harner
6. 'I Don't Want to Discuss It' Little Richard
7. 'A Little Bit of Something' Little Richard
8. 'Hide nor Hair' Earl Grant
9. 'I Miss You, Baby' Marv Johnson
10. 'Help Yourself' Billy Butler

Former Casino DJ Dave Evison's Top Ten Wigan Sounds

1. 'Country Girl' Vicki Baines
2. 'Strange Neighbourhood' Imaginations
3. 'Put That Woman Down' John Leach
4. 'It's the Little Things' Patti and the Emblems
5. 'Dance Dance Dance' Casualeers
6. 'Up and Over' Jay Traynor
7. 'Packin' Up' Damon Fox
8. 'You Left Me' Admirations
9. 'What Can I Do' Billy prophet
10. 'Give Up Girl' Connie Questell

Dave Evison's Top Ten Reactivated Oldies

1. 'I Can't Make It Any More' Spyder Turner
2. 'I Love Her So Much It Hurts' Majestics
3. 'You Lie So Well' Marie Knight
4. 'Move On Up' Curtis Mayfield

5. 'Sweeter Than The Day Before' Valentinos
6. 'Surprise Party For Baby' Vibrating Vibrations
7. 'Call Me' Eddie Bishop
8. 'Talking 'Bout Me Baby' Mighty Marvellows
9. 'A Lot Of Love' Homer Banks
10. 'Tightrope' Inez and Charlie Foxx

Steve Hallewell of Hoddlesden, near Darwen, Lancs. (formerly of Clitheroe) gives his Casino Top Ten

1. 'You Can't Come Home Again' P J Proby
2. 'It's Better To Have' Don Covay
3. 'One Way Out' Martha Reeves and the Vandellas
4. 'Time' Edwin Starr
5. '100 Pounds Of Pain' Lenny Welch
6. 'Girl Watcher' The Occasions
7. 'Job Opening' The Del Larks
8. 'Seven Day Lover' James Fountain
9. 'Girl Across The Street' Moses Smith
10. 'My Heart Needs A Break' Linda Jones

Dave Frearson (Podge) of Chorley, gives his Casino Top Ten

1. 'I Travel Alone' Lou Ragland
2. 'You Didn't Say A Word' Yvonne Baker
3. .I Just Can't Live My Life' Linda Jones
4. 'Too Darn Soulful' Morris Chesnut
5. 'Landslide' Tony Clarke
6. 'Hold On, Help Is On The Way' G Davis and R Tyler
7. 'Stick By Me Baby' Salvadors
8. 'Do I Love You' Frank Wilson
9. I Ain't Going Nowhere' Junior Walker
10. 'Tainted Love' Gloria Jones

Appendix

Useful Contacts

♣ Appendix: Useful Contacts

If this book has brought you out of Northern Soul hibernation, or if you want to see for yourself what this crazy underground scene is all about, here are just a few useful details for you.

Goldmine Records: PO Box 4, Todmorden OL14 6DA
Kent Records: 46–50 Steele Road, London NW10 7AS

Manifesto: 01452 300894

Blackburn All-nighters: 01902 652214
100 Club All-nighters: 0171 636 2622
Keele All-nighters: 01782 835235

STOP PRESS All-nighters set to return to Wigan at the Cricketers, Poolstock.
Details: 01942 826060

The authors and all associated with the Casino feel astonished that the Casino's contribution to the social history of Wigan has never been properly recognized. So what we suggest is this: there should be a Wigan Casino exhibition at Wigan Pier, which draws hundreds of tourists every weekend. Surely the council must realize the role the Casino played in putting their town on the map. But they need convincing. If you have enjoyed this book please do all us soul lovers a big favour and write to the Director of Leisure, Wigan Metropolitan Leisure Department, Trencherfield Mill, Wallgate, Wigan, Lancs. Just state that you think there should be a permanent exhibition in Wigan, dedicated to the Heart of Soul, and ask why we can't have one. Maybe one day they will realize what fools they have been.